795, AD

D0953112

How to Change Colleges:
Notes on Radical Reform

Other Books by HAROLD TAYLOR

On Education and Freedom
Art and the Intellect
The World as Teacher
Students Without Teachers:
  The Crisis in the University
Art and the Future

Editor and Co-Author
Essays in Teaching
The Humanities in the Schools

Editor
The Idea of a World University

How to Change Colleges: Notes on Radical Reform

HAROLD TAYLOR

Holt
Rinehart and
Winston

New York
Chicago
San Francisco

Copyright © 1971 by Harold Taylor

All rights reserved, including the right to reproduce
this book or portions thereof in any form.

Published simultaneously in Canada by Holt, Rinehart
and Winston of Canada, Limited.

Library of Congress Catalog Card Number: 71-148044

First Edition

SBN (Hardbound): 03-086361-9
SBN (Paperback): 03-086360-0

Printed in the United States of America

LB
2322
.T29

Contents

34055

Author's Note

How to Change Colleges: Notes on Radical Reform is a sequel to *Students Without Teachers: The Crisis in the University,* published in May of 1969, and is intended as a practical book or operating manual on how to put educational changes into effect. It came out of the experience of teaching, lecturing, and arguing on the campuses last year about the ideas I have been advocating in *Students Without Teachers* and elsewhere, and therefore goes back to the philosophy and main points of the previous book. I thought I should say in advance that any repetition is intentional.

HAROLD TAYLOR

Holderness, N. H.
October, 1970

Introduction

After spending last year on the campuses in the middle of the campus troubles and student unrest it seemed to me that the main reason the problems of unrest grew worse instead of better over the year was the failure of the colleges and universities to join with the students either in their opposition to the war, racial injustice, and the repressive attitudes of the government, or in the efforts the students were making to reform their own education. By students I do not mean the bombers and the violent ones. I mean the mass of students who have simply decided that they will no longer accept the conditions imposed on the country by those in power, and have acted publicly against them. Instead of taking an attitude of moral and intellectual support, the universities in most cases have treated the activist students as at best a nuisance and at worst a menace to the true mission of the university.

The universities finally did come around, when the combination of Cambodia and the murders at Kent State and Jackson State set off a national student revolt which even the President could not ignore. But in the interim, most remained aloof from the student cause, apprehensive, tentative, or downright hostile. What the students were trying to do was never fully understood because it became confused with sporadic acts of campus violence whose origins were in the undercurrents of violence in the country as a whole and which suddenly surfaced for all to see at Kent State and Jackson State. It was a violence imposed by the state against its citizens, the kind the whites have imposed against the blacks, and it breeds counter-violence of the kind we have been getting.

But the May student revolt had serious educational effects. The 1,500,000 students who were involved made the universities and the country pay attention to the consequences of their own actions and take the students

seriously as a force for political and social change. Without the students the intimacy of the connection between
a war policy which uses guns to impose American political aims abroad and a domestic policy which uses guns
to kill our own sons and daughters on behalf of the same
aims would have gone unnoticed, or if noticed, would have
been ignored. The students would not stand for it, no
matter who else would. They refused to believe that political power in a democracy comes out of the barrels
of guns.

The revolt also had a deeply educational effect in redefining the mission of the university. The debates about
whether or not the universities have a responsibility for
political, social, and moral action became literally academic. Overnight the universities and colleges began
taking such action by sending students and faculty members to Washington and taking responsibility for the education of the communities around them on the issues of
peace and war. Policies about class attendance, examinations, grading, and the content of university learning—
policies which had seemed immoveable for years ahead—
were changed in a matter of days. The tragedy in the
death of the innocents had changed the mood of the campuses from the dispirited acceptance of the impossibility
of change into one of constructive action to make the
changes happen.

What happens next will depend on whether the universities have finally accepted responsibility for taking the
students seriously, and whether they are now prepared
to serve as centers of creative thought and action for
meeting the problems of the students and their society.
The debate about whether or not they should is over. The
force of events and of student concern has settled that.

But it should not be necessary for an Asian country to
be invaded and American students killed before the university community addresses itself to the issues which
engage the minds and moral intelligence of the American

student body. Nor should it be left to the students to summon up the energies, ideas and social force to make educational reforms which the universities should have been making years and years ago.

There is a deep irony in the fact that the reform movement on the campuses has its main thrust in the agitation and criticism of students, and that they have been met with a mixture of sympathy, amused tolerance, scepticism, aloofness, opposition, and repression. Faculty members and educators should be at least as interested in education and social change as students, their parents, politicians, and government officials. It is odd, on the face of it, that it seems not to have occurred to educators that one obvious way to cure student unrest is to deal directly with the social and educational problems which are causing the unrest. The students are the ones who are restless, and one of the basic reasons for their restlessness, among all the others, is the lack of social content, relevance, and sense of purpose in the education they are given.

If the educators do not wish to be serious about making the university into a place where students can live a rich, rewarding, and lively intellectual life—an engaged life that commits them to the cause of mankind—they should move over and give the students a chance to invent their own university. Some of the students are already trying to do that, and they need help. This book is about how to give it to them.

1. The Virtues of Unrest

In the long run there are just two ways of dealing with the problems of student unrest—through education or repression. So far we have not tried education. We have kept the educational and social system in an obsolete state and put modern children into it. When we find that as they become older and more intelligent they either oppose the system or reject it entirely, for reasons with which it is hard to disagree, we call that student unrest and look for ways to control the unrest rather than for ways to change the system. We remind the students that they are students, not yet ready for equality as citizens, that there are many reasons why the system cannot be changed, that there are many channels open to them for giving advice, making suggestions, sharing decisions, and that there is no excuse for making disturbances on or off the campuses simply to assert their own demands. Then when they make the disturbances, we start to change the system.

This inconsistency on the part of their elders has not been lost on the dissenting students. They have taken their clues for action from it and have been greatly encouraged by it because of the progress it has made possible. This is not a matter of apportioning blame to the elders and a special kind of innocent wisdom to the young. It is a matter of simple fact. Student unrest is the natural outcome of the forces of social disorder which afflict the society and its institutions, a society in which students have begun to contribute through their own efforts the kind of energy, talent, and idealism the country needs to restore itself to educational and social health. The students are at the beginning stage of a social movement, which if it is not taken with the seriousness it deserves, will find its own way of increasing the social tensions to such a point that some of the present problems will in fact become incapable of solution by means other than violence. In other words, if the answer given to student unrest is repression and guns in place of concern and reform, the limited campus violence of the past will increase to the level of a small civil war between youth and the elders.

What is at stake is not merely the solution of the immediate problems of student unrest as they keep flaring up from year to year. It is the solution to the problem of how American social institutions, including the colleges and universities, can respond imaginatively to the reality of the changes that have already taken place in the society. At its deepest level, the issue is a conflict in philosophy between those who see the forces of change as threats to the stability of the social order and those who see every society as a mixture of stability and change, with the most stable society defined as one in which change is accepted as a natural way of maintaining stability and creating a viable future. In such a society, the university is the nerve center of moral and social intelligence within the entire social organism. Its function is to anticipate the needs of the changing environment, and to educate the generations to meet those needs. If it does not take that as its function, it will be swept aside by the changes themselves.

This is the heart of the issue. When the American society, in a double state of complacency and turmoil, found its institutions put on trial by the revolutionary changes of the 1960's, the university was simply not ready for its testing. It had never thought deeply about its own place in the society, and although as a social institution it was clearly involved in the policies of social change by its tacit and explicit commitment to the support of the established order, it had made no preparation for its own future other than to seek alliances with money and to rally political support for carrying on a set of unexamined tasks.

Those who now deplore the attacks on what they refer to as the fragile structure of authority and freedom within

the university are late in discovering that the authority
is fragile because it rests on obsolete ideas about the nature of learning and the function of the university in
modern society. Any structure of authority rests upon its
constituency, and the college and university have been
acting as if their constituencies were their academic
elites, the federal government (including the military),
the foundations, private donors, the alumni, and the
state legislatures. In the public universities, boards of
regents, although either elected or appointed by governors
and mayors, have not, as is their responsibility, represented all the citizens, including students, in their membership or in their policy-making and management. They
have represented the most conservative and reactionary
elements in the society.

The students, except in rare instances, have never been
considered part of any of the constituencies, even though
they are the fundamental reason why universities exist at
all. Neither have the citizens, if by citizens are meant *all*
the citizens and not simply those of the white middle-class
majority. Even now, those who are poor and non-white
are not properly represented, either in the student bodies
or in the policy-making apparatus of the educational institutions. Such gains as have been made in this direction
have seldom come as a result of imaginative educational
planning by the university and by educators, but from
militant action by students and their allies.

Nor have the universities taken account of the fact that
the student is a citizen, with at least as much intelligence,
initiative, good will, and good sense as any other citizen of
whatever age, in some cases with a good deal more, since
the student is in some sense selected as a person with
enough intelligence to warrant spending time and money
on his further development. The student is the direct link
between the mass society and the intellectual elites and
technological experts clustered together in the universities.

He brings in the news from outside and takes back what he has learned. He comes straight out of the mass culture, where he has absorbed its major characteristics, into the middle of university life, and joins his fellow students there as a representative of the variety of points of view, strengths, and weaknesses of the society at large. If he insists on making his presence felt, if he demands educational and social change, he does so not only as a student with interests of his own in his own future, but as a representative of the interests of the society, black and white, poor and well-to-do. If he acts in a just cause and his actions are in the American tradition of speaking and acting boldly for the redress of grievances, he is in a position to be listened to and to raise the level of visibility of the issue on which he acts.

That has been proven over and over again during these past five years of the student protest movement. The students have seized the moral advantage in the issue of the war, racial injustice, democracy in education, and the protection of minorities. It is only when those among them have deserted the philosophy of non-violence and have substituted intolerance, threats and acts of violence that they have lost that moral advantage and are seen by the rest of the students and the public at large to have deserted action in the common welfare for action taken to further an ideological self-interest.

The opponents of the student movement, including those who are advising the White House not to worry about it too much because students form so minor a part of the electorate and don't have the votes, are making the mistake of thinking that politics is just vote-getting. They are also falling into the trap of thinking of students as students rather than as citizens who are in a strategic position to exert political and social influence because students—and youth in general—are a subject of deep interest to the country. They are the children of parents and there are a great many parents.

They exert influence not because they constitute a student class or an elite of those selected for higher levels of education, but because they represent a variety of social and cultural groups, many of which have never been taken seriously either by politicians or by educators. Since the mass media, including the films, book publishers, and the students' own media in radio and press on the campuses, will continue to be interested in students and their lives, the student movement has access to the public in ways which few other movements can ever have.

When in the next five years the number of educated American Indians, Chicanos, blacks, Puerto Ricans, and members of the under-classes in general has increased through the community colleges, the colleges, and the universities, we are going to find ourselves in a much different situation in the strength and potency of political leadership in the minority cultures. In the past, the effect of university education on minority students was to groom them to fit membership in the established order.

That is no longer the case. The minority students are going to college determined to change the established order so that it fits *them*. There is every sign that their influence in education will be to radicalize other students as well as themselves, and to act as major elements in producing educational and social change within the educational system itself.

One has only to think of the shift in the municipal colleges of New York City to an overdue policy of open enrollment after two weeks of a Puerto Rican boycott in 1969 to understand the latent political and social power of the student movement. One has only to think of the cultural changes in the United States produced by youth through the development of a rock culture, and the relationship between that and the theater arts, the mass media, the clothing industry, commercial publishing, and the record industry to see what can happen when the school and college generation of the next four years finds its feet and begins to move into other areas of the arts, education and politics.

Other critics of the student movement, of whom there are more than ever before, speak of the militants, the bomb-makers, the building-burners, and the disrupters as if they were the main elements in the movement. They are not and never have been. The advocates of violence have been successful in gaining their demands, closing down a university, or disrupting it so badly that it might as well have been closed, either because the issue on which they have acted has had the support of the student body or because an incident, either manufactured or accidental, has afflicted the campus with the brutality of the police or the national guard.

The parallel argument is made that militant and disruptive action not only will destroy the fragile structure of the university and discredit it in the eyes of the public, but that the student movement willfully use tactics of extremism when there are already channels open to the students for redress of grievances or for remedying whatever situation the protest involves. This is simply not so. The channels are already owned and operated by the administration and faculty; the student comes in the role of suppliant rather than educational equal; he steps on a moving train running down its own tracks.

Seven years after the Berkeley uprising, the American university and its system of control and instruction remains substantially the same. The few changes that have been made do not get to the heart of the matter, which again is the question of the role of the university in contemporary life, including, first of all, the life of the student. The basic system remains untouched, and in the words of Robert H. Atwell, then Vice Chancellor of the University of Wisconsin, three days before the bombing of the U.S. Army Mathematics Research Center there, "Those who share power in the university are remote, aloof, and defensive. They have accommodated the forces of reaction to the point where I believe they have lost the confidence of a majority of the actively concerned students of all political persuasions."*

When the student movement is analyzed accurately, the crucial factor turns out to be this loss of confidence by the majority of concerned students in the intention and ability of those in power to correct injustices and make reforms. A survey of a cross-section of 560 student leaders by the League for Industrial Democracy in the spring of 1970 showed a striking response to the question of whether the students agreed with the following statement:

> Material affluence and the façade of democracy have made the majority of Americans incapable of understanding or working for meaningful social changes. Precisely because of the charade of freedom, we live under the most oppressive kind of social system—subtle though it may be.

Fifty-four percent of the student leaders recorded agreement, thirty-six percent disagreement. The statement was deliberately constructed to capture the general spirit and tone of New Left rhetoric. The fact that it gained a positive response from fifty-four percent of those surveyed gives to educators and anyone else who cares to become interested, the basis on which to think and act. The restoration of confidence is itself a subtle and complicated matter, and it cannot be achieved by the production of more studies of the causes of disorder, and unrest, or by the appointment of more faculty committees to study the university system and its curriculum.

It can only be achieved by specific actions and serious changes in the system, taken boldly and swiftly, and taken not because of the threat of more violence, but because of a commitment to the quality of education and life on the American campuses and in the American community. It must be understood that the student who is a radical activist is simply a student who has gone one stage further

* Quoted in the *National Observer*, August 31, 1970, p. 4.

than most of the other students. The students are not being led by nihilists and anarchists. They are being led by
the force of events and the reality of contemporary America, and at this moment in history they are being forced
into opposition to most of what America now stands for.
The fact is that they have expressed that opposition in
recent years through non-violent, peaceful and orderly
protest, on the campuses, in the cities and in Washington.
Protests that have involved personal injury and/or property damage, or any other incidents which could be called
violent, have made up less than seven percent of the thousands of student demonstrations in the past five years.
The largest proportion of such incidents has occurred not
through premeditated plans but through a combination of
circumstances usually having to do with the violence of
police action.

2. The Dismal Year

What I am saying about student unrest does not come from what so many people now call a soft attitude toward students, nor from general notions taken from the press, the mass media, and the literature of the student revolt. It comes from a hard attitude to the seriousness of the student problem after working directly with students, faculty members, administrators, politicians, radicals, liberals, moderates and activists of all kinds, on and off the campuses. On the basis of what I have learned over the years, I would say that we have now reached a point in American educational history when unless the colleges and universities take up the cause of the students in social and educational reform and work out ways of restoring their confidence and our own in what can be done to change the system, the influence of the universities on the national life may very well be destroyed, not by the students but by the effects of their own inadequacies.

By taking up the student cause I do not mean placating students or giving in to threats. That would be a quick way to lose their confidence at a time when students are looking for some show of serious principle. I mean holding to the principles of peace, racial equality, and social justice and working with students as partners in making the necessary changes in the universities to put them on the side of those principles.

After describing the intelligent and direct way in which the students, faculty, and administration at Princeton University met the campus strike crisis of last May in a spirit of unity, Professor Lawrence Stone of the Princeton faculty had this to say:

Make no mistake about it, these and many other political efforts of students and faculty should not be treated lightly. The first "Children's Crusade" ended in political annihilation and bloodshed in Chicago. If the second goes the way of the first, if the politicians refuse to listen and drastically

to change national priorities, the depth of despair among
the young and among the intellectuals is frightening to
contemplate.*

I agree. It *is* frightening to contemplate, as are its consequences. During the past year, I have found more often
than not among the most serious people on the campuses
—the ones who have been trying hardest to come to terms
with themselves in this society—a general mood of despair. It is a despair rooted in reality, not in literary history, and at the heart of it is a feeling of futility that
nothing can be done through education, politics, social
action, or personal commitment to rebuild a society which
has lost its way and can find no clear path to its own
future.

What I have found, against my will and inclination,
goes much beyond the general tone of genteel cynicism in
the usual style of the academy and beyond the common
frustration of social reformers, radicals, and activists
with the obstacles and complications put in their way as
they work for social change. The new mood seems to have
come from the cumulative effect, day after day, of large
and small betrayals and disappointments, the biggest of
which is the necessity of coming to terms with the brutal
fact that the war continues and that the spirit of war-
making continues to prevail. It goes from there to the
stark realization that the present government has no
great or ideal enterprise in mind for the American people
or for the world, no large and magnanimous intention of
curing the problems of race, poverty, and social inequality.
Instead it is conducting a holding operation to placate
white racists, dampen protest, support the capitalist system, repress the radicals, and to contain those ideas and
energies which might, if released, liberate the country
into a new beginning.

Whether or not the mood of despair is fully accepted,

* *New York Review*, June 18, 1970.

it grows from these roots and affects everything it touches. What it comes down to is a loss of faith in the capacity and willingness of the society to change its institutions without violence. Once that faith is lost, there are any number of consequences. One of these is the development of a new set of political emotions going from moral indignation, cynicism, withdrawal, and fear to hatred, rage, and nihilism, depending on the circumstances and temperament of those who have become disaffected. This is what is at the bottom of the entire range of phenomena now referred to as student unrest. At its deepest level, it is a metaphysical unrest of this historical period in which everything is being revalued and transvalued—including ideas of government, art, sex, education, morality, the future, and the idea of civilization and of man himself.

At other levels it is much less dramatic or intense. It is unrest in the sense of restlessness, discontent, and a generalized unease. Little of this could be traced to self-conscious despair, since in order to become desperate about a situation it is necessary to have given up hope, and most students have not yet become desperate in that sense. What they *have* given up is the hope that the universities will change unless students take strong and militant action, and they have lost confidence in the leadership of educators.

Others among them are restless because they are bored by their education, and their interests have turned toward political and social action because in it there is a feeling of being alive and in touch with the world and oneself, a feeling that is not to be had in the endless series of classroom exercises they go through week by week. Others among the blacks and minority groups are restless because the university environment is unnatural to them; it was designed for the white middle-class. What the black critics have to say about the regular curriculum and its irrelevance to their lives is perfectly true, even more true in their case than in the case of whites. When this is added to the feelings in the black community of unified unrest and antagonism to a white-controlled society and its white-controlled universities, it produces its own political energies for social and educational action.

For others among the whites, the unrest comes from the realization that they have had the privileges of the white American, and that the system is rigged against the rest. They have become politically self-conscious as they read about the place in America of the white well-to-do and they learn constantly about themselves as students from television documentaries, magazine articles, newspapers, films, and each other. Theirs is an unrest developed partly through their unwillingness to remain typed as privileged whites: they feel a special need to act because they have the privileges.

In some cases they feel the stigma of privilege so deeply that it creates a sense of guilt in not being black, oppressed and from Harlem. Sometimes this leads to deliberate efforts to cultivate the good opinion of the blacks in whatever political operation they may be running and to outdo the blacks in their antagonism to white society as a way of showing allegiance to a common cause.

At another level, and in the hands of radical activists, black or white, the mood of despair produces the moral and emotional justification for violent revolution and for the destruction of political democracy and its institutions by any available means. It need not be argued whether such a revolution in America could be successful, when the power at the moment is all on the counter-revolutionary side. But it can stop the society from functioning in its present terms. The revolutionary mystique can and does affect the status of the established order, since it is capable of drawing an increasing number of liberal and moderate activists into implacable opposition to that order. "We are summoned to act in unison with our friends," said Father Daniel Berrigan from the underground in the summer of 1970, "to join in a conspiracy, in jeopardy, in illegal non-violent actions, to hotten up the scene, wherever we are." In practice this can mean non-violent action in tacit support of violence. But more than that, it can mean a new gathering of forces to compel the established order to make the changes it has to make if it is not to be continually plagued by social disorder and the disintegration of its own institutions.

A statement comparable to Father Berrigan's comes from the President of the National Student Association, David Ifshin, a fraternity member and a cadet in the Reserve Officers' Training Corps at Syracuse University before he became the leader of a sit-in and a student strike against the Cambodian invasion. "Violence on the campus is a myth," says Ifshin. "Most of the violence is by police and National Guardsmen against students. When you don't have any other alternative, violence happens. I never have been involved in violence myself and I hope I never will . . . but I don't condemn it, I don't deplore it. I understand why it is happening." *

In the minds of a large section of the student liberals and moderates there is, along with scepticism about the social system, a latent or overt sympathy with the black and white revolutionaries as they defy the courts and the established order. In the minds of others, disbelief in the system justifies dropping out of it and leaving the field to those who want to stay in and fight for the spoils. The prevailing mood in the student movement is one of opposition to America and the feeling that if you are not in opposition there is something wrong with you.

In the past I have been willing to look at the disappointments and betrayals of history as a series of temporary setbacks which slow up the progress of the human race toward something better, and I have been able to find support for a belief in human progress by citing what has happened for the common good in this country and elsewhere when dedicated people went to work to change the

* Washington *Post*, August 26, 1970.

course of history. Although it has been chastened and modified by practical experience, I still hold that belief along with its corollary that a society can be changed, among other ways, by what is done in its educational institutions. But during the past year on the campuses, I found myself for the first time since the McCarthy-style attacks of the 1950's, continually on the defensive, contradicted and confronted by disbelievers and sceptics. I was accused of hope and faith when I should have been embracing depair and frustration.

I found that there was general agreement in the schools and colleges about the changes that needed to be made, but with the agreement went a host of reasons why they could not or would not be carried out. Among the reasons given were lack of money, inertia in the faculty, anger in the electorate and alumni, disruption by the students, lack of leadership in the administration, and a general confusion about the mission of the university.

I found myself being told that you cannot change the society by anything you do in the university, and that in any case, to change the society is not the university's business, no matter what the reformers and students say. The university exists to advance and disseminate knowledge. It should not involve itself in the political problems of the society; its task is to remain apart from politics and to preserve the academic freedom of the faculty against the attacks made on it by a mixture of radicals, right-wing politicians and a philistine public. It should go on doing what it had always done. As for the state of mind of the universities themselves, Mr. Pusey of Harvard expressed a general sentiment when he referred to "the dismal year."

The radicals and liberals agreed with Mr. Pusey, but for different reasons. They pointed to the supremacy of the law and order advocates, the Black Panther repression, the Chicago trial, the continuation of the war, the

Agnew attacks on intellectuals and dissenters, the Nixon slow-down in desegregation, the punishment of the universities by state legislatures, the triumph of Reaganism, the emergence of the hard hats, and the defeat of the student reform movement. They wanted to know why I could remain optimistic in the face of all this.

I replied that it was not a question of optimism but of the necessity of action. I said that optimism was not a necessary ingredient of that action, that there were things to be done that simply had to be done and that we had only begun to uncover the resources with which to do them. I said that 1970 was a crucial year that started with Woodstock in August of 1969 and went on to the October fifteenth and November fifteenth Moratorium days, then to the April twenty-second Earth Day, and ended with the student spring revolt after Cambodia, Kent State, Jackson, and Augusta; that changes long overdue were beginning to be made with a new coalition of students, blacks, parents, moderates, liberals, intellectuals, administrators, senators, and congressmen; and that the real issues of national policy were at last being tackled. I pointed out that the center of most of the positive action was on the campuses, and that the Nixon administration had at last been forced to recognize the political and social power located there.

My replies did little to dispel the general gloom. I found that quite a few of the students who had started projects in reform—experimental colleges, free universities, student-initiated courses—were discouraged halfway through the year because the students who were working with them got busy on other things and subsided back into the system. Other students decided that the faculty and administration were going so slowly through endless committees and study groups that they would be graduated and gone before anything useful or interesting could happen. Having become members of faculty and administrative committees, other students found themselves talked to death by faculty members, bored by the content of the discussions, appalled by the time it all took, neutralized by inclusion in the governing system.

Most of the radicals argued that nothing could be done about social, political or educational reform through regular channels in either the society or the university, since the university was simply an extension of the coercive apparatus of the society. They informed me that the United States as an imperialist power has set out to control the world by military and economic force, that the educational system is being used to support that aim, that students are victims under the controls of the system, that capitalist democracy makes all of this an historical necessity. It therefore followed that the system must be broken up at whatever point possible by whatever means, starting with the university. The way to do that was to set fire to buildings, plant bombs, break windows, trash the campus and community, disrupt classes, interfere with speeches, fight the police if possible, and to insult and disrupt the faculty and administration. When reminded that this would not produce the changes they had in mind but only infuriate the public, alienate supporters, and encourage the growth of militant right-wing coalitions against the revolution, they made the familiar reply: If we have to have fascism before we get rid of what we have now, then that's the way it will have to be.

The liberals and the moderates did not accept the doctrine whole, but they accepted its emotional and political overtones. We have been brought up to believe that this is an honest, democratic, humane society, they said. Then we begin to discover that we have been told a pack of lies, and that war, racism, and oppression are the natural expressions of what America really stands for. As patriots for the kind of America we believe in we therefore have to go into opposition to the present country, since the way the system works, there is nothing you can do to change it except to refuse to play its games. That is what the radi-

cals are saying and doing, and the only difference between
them and us, say the liberals and moderates, is that they
go farther in their opposition, while we either get out of
the system or stay in it and hate ourselves for playing its
games.

Their position was strengthened last year by the declared anti-intellectual and anti-democratic biases of the
present government and the attacks on the intellectual
community by Mr. Agnew. The more Mr. Agnew talked
about rotten apples in the barrel, about an effete corps of
impudent snobs, about liberal dissidents who needed curb-
ing, and about the need for control of the mass media, the
more the opposition groups among the students coalesced
against authority of all kinds. To be attacked by name by
Mr. Agnew was a guarantee of university-wide support
for whatever views one expressed; being called bums by
Mr. Nixon gave the radicals the status of cultural heroes.

On many campuses the effect of the Nixon-Agnew-
Mitchell approach to intellectual and political freedom
was to give credibility to all efforts to defy authority, no
matter what form they took. Added to this was the effect
of the My Lai revelations in deepening the war resistance
and increasing the antagonism toward the whole of the
government's policies, including the policy of cutting
budgets for higher education and taking a legal rather
than a moral view of the problems of desegregation. Then,
of course, came Cambodia and the murder of students,
proving everything about foreign policy and repression
that the radicals and liberals had been saying, shocking
citizens of good will everywhere, on and off the campuses.
It was an unhappy, negative time.

When I argued with the radicals, especially the anarchists among them, that there were ways of changing the
system without destroying it and gave evidence of the
ways it had been done and could be done both from the
outside and the inside, I won no assent, but only angry

replies. They had both a psychological and a political need to deny any possibility in the system. In the case of some of the angrier ones, it was clear that they had to have a continuous supply of hatred of America as fuel for their political engine. Without the hatred the engine would not run, and anyone whose hatred against the United States was anything less than complete was counted an enemy.

I can also report that the kind of authoritarianism and intolerance which marked the later stages of SDS tactics and policies when they were active on the campuses continues among relatively unorganized fringe groups and anarchists within the New Left. Whether it is called in polite terms an absence of civility or denounced as the overthrow of academic freedom, it does have the effect where it exists of poisoning the intellectual atmosphere and making serious public debate and discussion of politics impossible. Even when it does not block debate completely as in the cases where speakers are prevented from speaking through invasions of the platform or shouting and heckling, it often introduces such a tone of rancor and malice through the invective, that no real exchange of ideas can take place at a meeting. The enemies of liberalism want immediate action on their demands wherever they go, and they are capable of putting so much static in the communication system that all the messages become garbled if not jammed.

It is a situation of great difficulty, since a handful of such students can in fact take all the seriousness and mutual trust out of a public meeting without breaking any laws but merely by destroying the ease of relationship between the audience and the speakers or between those whose ideas differ. I am not talking about gentility or even civility. I have been at enough political meetings and rallies to know that the best of them are those in which the people there are completely uninhibited in what they say and how they say it.

This is something different. It is the deliberate effort to

defeat the method by which political issues can be settled
through debate and democratic process, an attack on liberal democracy through destroying its instruments, and it
catches the fair-minded liberal and moderate students and
faculty off guard. They want to go on defending the militants and their right to speak, to agitate and take extreme
measures, up to and including the point at which the liberals themselves are blotted out of their own discourse.
Liberal students who are inexperienced in politics and
radical action often find themselves supporting the right
of militants to shut off the opinions of anyone who dis-
agrees with them, or if not supporting that right, supporting the right of the offenders not to be disciplined
after they have accomplished the shutting off.

This kind of confusion about liberalism and its meaning
in action is one of the fundamental weaknesses in the educational and political thinking of students and faculty
alike. On the student side, it has roots in the fact that students in high school and college have never learned the
rules of the democratic game and the meaning of politics
in action. They have been protected from political ideas of
any serious kind, especially in the radical sector, and their
natural environment for political action is more like an
American Legion prize-giving day or a Rotarian luncheon
than a serious meeting of a political party.

Since the students have been kept in ignorance and
have never learned to engage in real politics as it is actually practiced, they don't know when the practices are
destructive and malicious. Since they have never before
confronted the political ideas of the radical movement,
they find it very hard to know what to do with them and
with their advocates, many of whom are their friends.
The dilemma then is that while they refuse to accept the
simplistic notion proposed by Mr. Nixon that radicals are
bums, they have no political or intellectual equipment to
meet the radical arguments with counter-arguments based
on equally valid premises.

Faculty members have some of the same difficulty, especially those who are liberal minded, although the conservatives have the same trouble in a different way—they are appalled by the roughness of the language and the disrespect shown to them by the political roughnecks who have merely brought to the campuses the conventional style of the politics of the longshoremen, the Teamsters' Union, the construction workers, and the New Left. In the case of the liberal faculty members, their intelligence and liberal attitudes lead them to accept the right of militants to speak and act forcefully. But without any prior experience with the rough and tumble of New Left politics or of practical politics as it is carried on among street workers and organizers, they quite often back away from the question of civil rights and free speech by extending the limits of permissible behavior so far that all forms of political action, no matter how destructive, are equally condoned.

Liberal faculty members were not ready for the assault when it came, nor was the structure of authority of which they are a part. Since that structure excluded the students, the dilemma for the liberal arose in the fact that his sympathy was with students who were "fighting for their rights," yet without some principle of accountability or limit to permissible behavior under a code of due process, it was impossible to say what was a fight for a right and what was a planned program to defeat the possibility of democratic education.

Having established a psychological and political foothold, the militants then discovered how vulnerable the system was, and how, with a comparatively minor degree of forcefulness (sit-ins, demonstrations, non-negotiable demands, etc.), they could produce changes which otherwise would have been impossible. The fact that most of the changes were of a kind which should have been made years ago then lent strength to their movement. That strength comes from the rise in expectation of change which raises the general level of militancy and the feeling

of comradeship among all those who go into opposition.
Until the structure of authority is reconstituted to give
students a genuine part in making educational policy decisions and redefining their role in the university, the
present structure will continue to be vulnerable.

I found among the faculty members and administrators
with whom I talked a great deal more understanding than
in previous years of the legitimacy of student protest and
its links to the spiritual and social malaise in the country
at large, and much more willingness to set to work on the
problems. What bothered me most was that too few faculty members were prepared to go to the roots of the educational issues and to make radical revisions in the whole
conception of what the students needed and how best the
university could arrange its affairs to meet their needs
and the needs of the wider community around them.

Part of the resistance to deeper thinking about the issues came from the polarization of the university into
antagonized groups: students organizing to demand, defeat, and impose; faculty members organizing to defend,
sustain, and adjudicate; with the administration in an un-
easy balance between outside pressures for more authority and control of the students *and* the faculty, and the
legitimate demands for cultural and political freedom
made by students and faculty against the outsiders.

Another part of the resistance to change came from the
sheer fragmentation of the internal university community. This had to do not only with the internal units of
the departments and the various schools of arts and sciences, technology, business, medicine, architecture, law,
education, and the rest, but with the lack of sensitive and
sympathetic relationships between the university and
state legislatures, boards of regents, administrators, faculty, students, and community leaders. In some cases I
found each of these groups frozen into attitudes toward
one another that made the posture of antagonism the

norm, with no sense of common purpose in improving the quality of life either within the university or outside it.

None of the groups except the students seemed willing to look the problem straight in the eye and say serious changes have to be made, it is not a question of prerogatives or existing structures, there is something fundamentally wrong with the way we are educating students and it is not possible to go on as we have in the past. Nor is it possible for the faculty to go on saying what has always been said, that the university *is* the faculty, and that what the faculty says and does is what decides what a university is and should be.

This has never been true in the past, it has merely been asserted by faculty members on their own behalf as they have organized themselves into a position of academic power. There are any number of others who have had a hand in defining and redefining the university. In the final analysis, the university is its students at work with their teachers, and their teachers have a joint obligation with the students to design an environment that is rich and nourishing in the quality of ideas and experiences it has to offer. The faculty members are now discovering that whatever they may think of their place as the policy-makers of the university community, that place is being altered daily by what the students are thinking and doing.

They are also discovering that they have lost much of their capacity to influence students. This is partly because most of the students are kept busy with their own affairs and do not want to be influenced, or are among the activists and militants who want to do all the influencing themselves. But it is mainly because, in the present system, the faculty member in the eyes of the student has become a non-person who is hired by the university to teach academic courses the student must take in order to graduate. Most students have never thought about the system, nor could they describe what it is. Until lately they have simply gone through it, doing what is necessary, with the pro-

fessor seen as part of the general equipment of the institution, a person to be dealt with according to the ground
rules.

In the case of the university crises in which demonstrations, disruptions, riots, or the invasion of buildings have
raised the issues of student rights and student discipline
as against faculty prerogatives and responsibilities, it
used to be assumed that the faculty could act as a mediat-
ing force between the students and their target—the university administration. As the years of protest have con-
tinued, this has become less and less the case. In situations
of conflict, militants see the faculty as part of the system
they are attacking, bound to it by tenure and self-interest,
just as much the opponents of the students as the administration, the board of regents or the state legislature.

During the year, I had my own taste of abuse from militants, sometimes to my astonishment. I discovered that
as far as some of them were concerned, it was not enough
for me to hold serious radical views on political and social
issues, views which on the whole corresponded with their
own. Unless the views were expressed in exactly their
terms, and identified the United States as the enemy of
mankind, the best words to describe me were "liberal
fascist" or "white pig." The slightest deviation from their
curious gnarled position was enough to place me in the
enemy camp. Much of the time this was just a bad-tem-
pered effort at bullying the teacher and showing him that
whatever he stood for was a monstrous fraud.

Most of the militants were much less hostile, and I had
the feeling that they actually felt sorry that a man in my
position who might be expected to know better turned out
to be so unaware of the grim nature of the American situation. The implication was that I had become the Hubert
Humphrey of the intellectuals. Others were more blunt
and said that I held the views I did because I was part of
the system and was benefiting from it, that I was simply

telling my audiences and my students what they wanted to hear. To be optimistic about liberal democracy or about the possibility of change without violence was to be either a dupe or a propagandist for the system.

One trouble I found in many of the discussions was that the radicals, liberals, moderates, and conservatives alike had no other experience with a political or educational system with which to compare their own. They had no historical *or* contemporary examples. If I described the tragedy of the Czech student movement under Soviet occupation, or what had happened to the students under Mao and the Maoist policy of controlling the universities by peasants, workers, and soldiers, they construed this as anti-communist talk, the sort of thing liberals were always saying to divert attention from American imperialism and racism.

They simply put their experience of their country against mine and denied the validity of mine. They gave examples of repression from state legislatures, governors, boards of regents, deans, and college presidents, with repression often defined as anything that interfered with the actions of students in doing whatever they insisted on doing. They cited cases of faculty members being dismissed or not reappointed because they had introduced controversial materials into their teaching or had joined the students in their protests.

My reply was to say that of course these things were true, and that the struggle for a free society was a real one with real people put in real jails, that it went on every day in every country of the world, and that it went on in this country with more show of success for our side than in most others. It was up to them, to me, to everyone else who cared about the integrity of the free intellect, democracy, and social justice, not merely to complain about the system, but to work out counter-strategies against whoever and whatever was at fault. When I mentioned the gains we had made since the 1930's and 1950's in protecting the rights of students and teachers, especially since the 1950's when teachers could be dismissed for having once belonged to an organization that was later called subversive, this was taken as evidence that this country had always been repressive and would go on being that way.

I finally got down to bedrock. I said: You are dealing almost completely in abstractions. You have set up the United States as an abstraction and are heaping on it all your personal frustrations. You set up an ideal state in your head, an imprecise ideal state in which everyone has everything he needs and wants, but you don't describe how it is all arranged to make that possible. Then you blame the United States, the taxpayers, the university presidents, the faculty, your parents, Richard Nixon, Spiro Agnew, and "the system" for not giving you the state you have in your head. Take your mind off Mr. Nixon for a while and get down to business. If you are serious you will have to deal with the reality of your own self, your friends, your family, your community, your world, and you will have to know how you are linked, outside yourself, to all the others who make up your society. Otherwise you keep deluding yourself that it is always somebody else's fault or the fault of some sort of abstraction called the United States.

Their reply most often was to return to an attack on the system, to say once more that it was inherently repressive, and that if they worked within it in the ways I was proposing, they were being co-opted, with no hope of ever changing what was wrong. I was again accused of believing in progress and other liberal fallacies. I repeated my beliefs that we *could* change the system, by working both outside and inside it, and we were back to the question of their despair and my hope. It was hard going, but on the whole not as hopeless as my description may make it seem. These are the real philosophical and practical issues with which educators have to deal, and unless they are argued in the reality of the students' political context, they go by default.

It seems to me that the radical students have not faced enough serious intellectual response and that too often faculty members have turned away from them because their style of arguing is so fierce and their convictions so intense and so dogmatically expressed. They have therefore had an intellectual field day in which they have awarded themselves all the prizes. Discussions with students who deny the entire basis on which one's argument rests and then simply return to a restatement of their own convictions are exasperating, especially when even the integrity of the motives for one's own belief is called into question.

But on the other side of exasperation lies some plain truth. If it is not possible to make a case for liberal democracy that is convincing to students in general and that can meet the system-breakers on their own ground, the issue of whether or not non-violent social change is possible *will* go by default. If it is not possible to demonstrate convincingly that liberalism and radicalism are parts of the same philosophy, and that radicalism is not the exclusive property of the bomb-throwers, there is little hope that students or educators can find the strategies and leadership they must have for producing non-violent change.

3. Radicalism and Liberalism in Education

In my case, the effect of the confrontations with the militants was to throw me back on my own resources and to force me back into questions I had thought were settled. I grew weary of the attacks on liberals and liberalism and the accusation that they and it were the enemy. The attackers were alternately blaming liberalism for everything from the war to Ronald Reagan and congratulating themselves that they had Reagan as the archetype of the capitalist monster.

If the Soviets take over Czechoslovakia is that because the idea of a liberal society has failed or because authoritarianism has won? If force is substituted for reason, among persons or among states, is that because reason has failed or because force has conquered and reaped its own rewards? We have a daily demonstration in Indochina of how force unrelated to social ideals defeats the purpose for which it is used.

The idea that liberalism is the chief enemy and the cause of all social failure was to me absurd. Certainly there are persons who identify themselves as liberals and who have failed, both in the politics of persuasion and in the ideology some of them have linked to their kind of liberalism. But how can liberalism fail when it advocates no universal ideology or political doctrine other than the mandate to treat other people as people and keep them from all possible harm? How could a philosophy which refuses to rely on force and violence to impose political goals do damage to the radical cause, except by winning converts to the idea that social change through non-violent means is possible? In which case the converts would be non-violent radicals, which is a perfectly proper thing for a radical to be.

27

The young radicals, white and black, who favor violence as the instrument of change, have staked out a claim for the entire territory of radical thought and action, when in fact they occupy their own corner of a cluttered terrain. When they come to questions of education, they rush at them with a single answer—overthrow the present curriculum with its white racist imperialist corrupt dishonest repressive capitalist content and put in ours.

There is nothing particularly radical about that kind of educational change, except in the method proposed for getting it accomplished. The educational program it would substitute for what we have now would be reactionary—a monolithic structure of ideas and beliefs to be used as indoctrination for a revolution to produce a society as yet undefined. It is an educational program that can be used as well by the right wing as by the left. Its content depends on the body of ideas chosen, not on the radical nature of the educational thinking.

A radical in education is one who extends the limits of the curriculum beyond any one set of ideas from anywhere and gives ultimate freedom to the individual psyche. A radical in politics who has a doctrine according to which all social and political questions must be answered becomes by necessity an educational reactionary. An example can be drawn from the political and social contribution the Black Panther Party is making to the political health of the country by producing genuine radicals whose politics and revolutionary spirit have their roots in the reality of black repression. But the Black Panther educational program, like the para-military structure of their organization, is designed to produce a single state of mind and a single body of ideas on behalf of a single aim. They could not afford to be radical in educational theory or practice and still hope to accomplish the purpose for which they are organized. I think the distinction has to be recognized.

Suppose we admit everything on the other side of liberalism. Mankind is greedy, scholars are ambitious, politicians are venal, schools are prisons, police are brutal, the world loves war, the colleges have failed, the universities are dehumanized, the world is run by gangsters, the weak are victimized, the society is adrift, the environment is polluted, hate is easier than love, and the bomb awaits. Anything anyone wants to say about the perversity of human institutions, the demonic in human nature, the hypocrisy of the United States, the Soviet Union, Spain or Jordan, is hereby granted and doubled.

Where does that leave us?

Exactly where we were, with nowhere to go. Unless, that is, we are prepared to accept the idea that the only way to deal with presumptive evil is either to submit to it or to conquer it by military force.

I am prepared to accept the fact that we may all go down together into various kinds of disaster. What I am not prepared to do is to believe that that is all there is, that only force can change the world, that we *have* to go down, that the demons will win. Even if they do, it would be an insult to accept defeat without a struggle, or even to believe that man does not have within himself the powers of his own redemption. It is time to muster the counter evidence, to say that the world can be changed, that there is a politics of love and humanity, and that the very simplest things a man can do are in the end the only things that matter.

These have to do with helping others to live and to grow by giving, in a total act of friendship, whatever of oneself might be useful to them. This is the inner meaning of liberal education. It is also the inner meaning of radicalism in education. The world's knowledge grows by the mutual help of students and their teachers, scholars and their colleagues, and the individual grows with the help of friendly allies. The school or college at its best is a community of friends who share common interests and mutual responsibilities and give to each other what no one could have by himself.

In this sense education at its best can and does change the world, since it changes people from what they were into something new, and the new in them is added to what presently exists. The degree and kind of change depend on the number and kind of the individuals involved. When there are enough individuals who have changed to liberal commitments, the society is changed in a liberal direction. Although the sociologists can eliminate the individual and speak legitimately of social, political, or economic forces at work to change society, and others can say that the necessities of history determine events, the forces themselves are generated by individuals, separately or in groups. It is a matter of the intensity of individual and group effort, the degree of commitment to a given set of ideas and beliefs, and the number and size of the groups involved. The institutions of education are therefore instruments of change, if they want to be; that is, if the teachers teach in such a way that their pupils learn to create their own lives in cooperation with others with a similar purpose.

Out of this comes a philosophy of education with a consistent set of principles. Whether the philosophy is called progressive, liberal, or radical depends on who is describing it and how far its principles are put into effect. It is radical in the sense that it means the complete revision of the way teaching is now carried on in the schools and colleges, since it puts the life of the child and the college student at the center of the curriculum and invents ways of teaching and learning which can liberate his intelligence, establish his identity, and join him together in a community of his fellows.

It is fair therefore to call the free school movement radical, since it goes back to the roots of learning and calls for the replacement of the formal curriculum with one developed by children and their teachers as they go along, without formal classes, testing, grading, units of hours, or assignments according to age or grade levels. It is also accurate to call the idea of schools without walls a radical educational concept, since it takes children and young adults into the community and into the streets, into the reality of their own society and teaches them how to use the world as their campus. It does not necessarily follow that because an educational idea is radical or a program is radical it is necessarily better than anything else. It depends what the idea is, how it works in practice, on behalf of what aim.

Nor is radical education necessarily education by and for radicals. It depends on what a radical is radical about. Radical education goes back to the simple assumption that the aim of education in a free society is, in the old-fashioned words, to help all children everywhere to become what they are capable of becoming. This means that it works with their capacities and helps them to grow naturally as persons, not with the explicit intention of using them to build a strong society according to established social goals, but for the sake of each child. Since it is radical in the point of view it takes toward human nature and the necessity of building a humane society through education, it is therefore liberal and radical in its politics. Its logic demands that it come down on the side of the poor, the deprived and the disenfranchised, otherwise it could not devote itself to the welfare of each child.

When that is the aim, the society becomes strong by the multiplication of individual strengths and the unfolding of new characteristics in new combinations. An adult is a grown child, and at each stage of life each human is undetermined in his own nature. He is set in the pattern of his own life by what life has done to him, but there remains constantly the chance of doing something back.

That is the crucial question, what to do back, how to inject oneself into one's own life. To answer that question, and to be fully human, it is necessary for each person to rise to a certain level of self-consciousness, to know enough about himself and the conditions of his own existence, to know what to do with the person he is and the person he might become. There are hints in one's own nature that reveal oneself to others, and the best kind of teacher is one who is sensitive enough to be able to help the child and the adult to discover what they are.

That is why most educational systems and schools work so badly. They do not deal with the crucial question of how to create a life of one's own. Their work is all external and behavioral—they set out to equip the child and young adult with a ready-made psyche for use in a ready-made world, and count him a failure if he rejects the psyche prepared for him.

Accordingly, we do not lack a definition of the relation of education to society, or of the responsibility of the schools and colleges for their students. On one side stand the governments, the military, the police, the managers, and controllers of society with their supporters in the legislative bodies, making their arrangements according to their values, demanding of education a certain kind of human product. On the other side stand the teachers, the students, the artists, the scientists, the intellectuals, and the citizens concerned about peace, justice and the quality of human life. There is traffic between the two sides, depending on the political and economic structure and the degrees of its freedom, but at a given point the lines are drawn and the teachers and students stand together in the cause of human liberation.

In a large sense, this is what the students are saying—that the universities belong on their side, on the side of humanity, and that the universities are *their* institutions, responsible, through the assertion of a collective will, for the encouragement and support of action in ideal causes, not merely for giving society what it wants and what it demands. The university exists for the creation of a rich and varied psychic life for all who are in it, and to deepen the human capacity for responding, enjoying, feeling, loving, knowing, acting, and imagining. If the university contradicts these purposes by its practices, it has gone over and joined the other side.

In becoming political and social activists, most students are searching through action for answers to questions of principle, and they are putting the university on trial as to where it stands on principle. Having refused to accept the day-to-day standards of the politicians and social managers who are making the policies and making history happen in their own way, the students are judging the worth of American culture and the worth of their own education by appealing to the sensibility of mankind.

> It is quite certain, that unless we can regulate our behavior much more satisfactorily than at present, we are going to exterminate ourselves. But as we experience the world, so we act, and this principle holds even when action conceals rather than discloses our experience. We are not able even to *think* adequately about the behavior that is at the annihilating edge. But what we think is less than we know, what we know is less than what we love, what we love is so much less than what there is. And to that precise extent we are so much less than what we are.*

What makes this country so slow to respond to its own best possibilities is that it has eliminated from its educational system most of the things that could teach the young to know what there is to love. By the age of ten or twelve, children have been taught to love their country, but not how to love its people, only its political institutions. They have learned above all to love success; even the love of their country depends on its success: whether it is first to the moon, wins its wars, has more bombs than the Soviet Union, and provides its people with more chances to make

* R. D. Laing, *The Politics of Experience* (New York: Pantheon Books, 1967), p. 32.

money. Mr. Nixon is the major contemporary exponent of that philosophy of success. As he has put it, he does not want the United States to lose the war, to become a "pitiful helpless giant," suffering "its first defeat in its proud 190-year history." By implication Mr. Nixon wants it always to win at whatever game it plays, to be a pitiless, *successful* giant.

The conditions of the society are now such that the children of the elites, the middle classes and the poor grow up in the same mass culture with everyone else, including their teachers and parents, and the mass culture educates them all, in and out of the schools and colleges. This means a great many things, among them the fact that we continue to develop people who are competitive about their own success and who accept the competitive system whole, inside and outside the schools and colleges, because it gives them a chance to get the social and material success they want. This is expressed in points scored in football games, number of dollars earned per year, batting averages, reading levels, I.Q. scores, body counts, grade point averages. Failure, the greatest punishment of all, is decided by lack of points.

In the case of the minority groups and the poor, even though they have never been taught to play the educational game and make points, they are still tested by how many points they make, in I.Q. tests, reading levels, and all the rest of it. The welter of research about learning to read and the quarrels about how to cure reading problems obscure the simple fact that children learn to read by reading, just as they learn to talk by talking and that they do both when the environment makes this natural.

But the schools and the colleges have not taken their mission as very much more than fitting out their students with the competitive skills to make their way in the society as it now exists. The idea that the education of the sensibility is the major task of the schools and colleges is remote from the minds of educators. They have therefore thought of the arts of life, including politics and social change, as tangential when in fact they are central. They have left no room in their schedules and their curricula for the practice of the arts themselves and for the discovery of the possibilities in human experience. The psychic environment of the institutions of education is extroverted, barren, and hostile to the imagination.

That is one of the things the present generation of high school and college students is discovering for itself. Many of them have found a more nourishing environment outside the educational system. Their hearts are in the youth culture while their bodies are in school. When they protest against the lack of relevance of the curriculum in which they are imprisoned, they are saying that the studies they are forced to carry out are unrelated to the problems of their own lives and their own society. But what they are also saying is that there is no spiritual, intellectual, or esthetic nourishment in the teaching and the learning. They are therefore turning to their own culture and its resources for the enjoyment of art forms and modes of experience which are simply unavailable inside the system.

Looked at from this point of view, the schools and colleges can be seen as institutions organized against the interests of those who attend—if by interests are meant the natural things the young wish to do, the things which can command their involvement simply because they enjoy them and believe in doing them. Beneath the surface of the acts of rebel students against their schools and colleges lies a feeling of resistance to anything official, to the idea that there is an official knowledge possessed by experts, that there is a standard culture. The student reformers say they want an education related to their lives. Many of them are not completely clear about what that is, except that it is not what they are getting. They want an education at a time in their lives when they are still groping for what kind of life they want and are trying themselves out in different ways to see what life is like. If their demands on society and its schools and colleges are often contradictory and inchoate, they could hardly be otherwise in a society which gives them a psychic and political environment full of contradictions and chaos.

They demand not that the schools and colleges become more like the society but that the division between life in the society and life in the school and college be shattered, that the educational plan take its beginning in the personal experience of the student with his own life in his own time. That is part of what the students mean by relevance. They are not saying that Plato is irrelevant. They are saying that philosophy professors and teachers of the humanities and social sciences who deal with Plato and other figures of intellectual history do not reach to the center of the issues with which Plato deals. For them the teaching does not become a source of insight into the actual mind of a man who lived with real problems in a real society. It becomes one more set of statements to be listened to. Without as yet knowing what it is their lives contain or what it is they truly want, they are certain that there is something worthy of their wanting, something more to be found than presently exists.

4. Violence and Educational Policy

To be worthy of student expectation, the university should be a beautiful open space for living and for changing one's life, for extending the boundaries of the self, a place where one is invited to make one's life out of the materials at hand with the help of teachers, artists, scientists, scholars, and other students. It should be one of the happiest places on earth, and it should be designed to make the earth a happier place. At this point it is not and there are many who rise to say that it can never be more than it is and in all probability will be less.

Enough has been reported on all sides to inform the public and anyone who will listen that student unrest has genuine causes that must be understood and dealt with before there can be much success in putting the unrest to creative use. Most of the attention has been given to the necessity of controlling violence. But so much attention has been given to the fact that the roots of unrest lie in the public problems and social disorder of this stage in the country's history that some of the simpler, and in many ways more fundamental, causes within the educational system itself are either overlooked or underemphasized. If the principal of a school or the president of a college is told that the causes of unrest lie in the war in Indochina, the race problem, social injustice, and the failure of electoral politics, he is likely to say: Thank you very much, but how do I keep my school open?

He can of course, along with his students and faculty, organize educational and action programs to work on the issues. But unless proposals for meeting the causes of unrest can be translated into practical things to do in his institution, all the causal analysis in the world will be of no help to him. He will understand that many of the things wrong with the society are also wrong with its educational

institutions and that there are specific responsibilities he
has in his own institution to work on them, no matter
how helpless he may feel about doing anything to change
the whole social order. You work where you are at what
you can do.

Since that is the case, the problem of violence on the
campus must be seen as a special problem produced by
special circumstances, which, although latent, did not
exist in previous years. There are no real precedents and
no body of practices. Unless the problem of campus violence is seen in the larger context of the structure of the
whole student community, there will be no satisfactory
answer to the question of what to do about it. Set aside
for a moment the burning and bombing of buildings. They
are criminal acts. The justification given by those who
commit the acts is that they have set out to damage in
any way they can the institutions through which the
United States imposes a brutal foreign policy and a repressive social order. This kind of argument is one which
could be made just as easily on the other side by John
Birchers, Ku Klux Klanners, and American Nazis. It
carries no serious weight with the student movement.

What it does carry is a feeling among students that the
violence is the inevitable result of a failure by the university and its client, the government, to act on behalf of
peace and justice. It was because the student body, the
faculty, and the administration at Yale University held a
common point of view about the role of the university in
supporting the cause of justice that the demonstrations
and rallies for the Black Panthers on the May first weekend of 1970 remained peaceful and non-violent. It was
because the same kind of unity was established, along
with a genuine role for students in university policy-making, that Princeton University emerged from the May
crisis with an imaginative program of political and educational action which had the backing of the whole university community.

The major campus crises from Berkeley to Kent State have arisen when the student body in sufficient numbers joined together in some form of collective unilateral action to make demands on the university or the government or both. Sometimes the take-over of buildings was involved, sometimes sit-ins, at other times disruption of classes. But the center of the crisis in each case lay in the fact that the student body, right or wrong, had come down on the opposite side of an issue in which the university was automatically involved whether it wanted to be or not.

Yet the student body, as of now, has had no real responsibility for making the policies according to which the issues can be resolved, nor has it been given the responsibility for finding the ways in which protest meetings and demonstrations can be made into vehicles for educational and social change. They therefore become vehicles for attack on the university and its administration, which in response, uses its security forces to keep order, and at a given point in the disorder, turns over the campus to the police or the national guard. The university is then bracketed with the police as sponsors of violence and the police usually oblige by displays of brutality that confirm the students' opposition to their own university.

All this is familiar ground, as is the tactic of some of the militant groups in doing their best to create a situation in which it is necessary to call the police and then to do everything they can to provoke the police into a pitched battle. What is not so familiar is the idea that if the student body were truly self-governing, the students who organize demonstrations would monitor their own meetings and take responsibility for keeping them non-violent through a system of marshals, as do the Black Panthers and many of the peace groups when they hold their rallies, parades, and meetings.

When 800 students meet in plenary sessions at the National Student Association annual congress, the speakers, advocates, and organizers are just as radical and vociferous as any of those who populate the campuses. But the students' demands must be made on themselves, not on a nearby building with administrators in it. They are their own administrators, the campus they occupy at the time of their congress is their campus and they are responsible for it. During the time of the 1969 crisis at Harvard, it was not until the administration had acted by calling the police and the campus was in turmoil that an all-student meeting was called, by the students, in which the student body took responsibility for its own affairs and made decisions about how to resolve the crisis. A university which took its students seriously would have called such an all-student meeting instead of calling the police, or would have asked the students to call the meeting to deal with issues it was their responsibility to resolve.

One of the results of having excluded students over the years from having anything to do with university policymaking is that they now look at the university, not as theirs, but as an organization run by boards, presidents, and the people the presidents hire. The split between the student body and the university is built in right at the start. Student governments do what they can to govern student affairs, usually at a primitive level, or as an advisory group. In most cases they are a minor part of the authority structure and have little to say about basic university policy. If they or any other student group on the campus want to change the institution, either through starting a student college or proposing a new curriculum, they end up in an adversary position.

For this reason I argue that in order to reach the problem of violence on campuses, we must start a great deal farther back, and not only put students on boards of regents and boards of trustees, but give them full responsibility for self-government on the campus and a position of equality with the administrative officers with whom they deal. The same kind of relationship should exist in the educational policy-making with the faculty.

To be quite practical about this, something else will have to be done in the big universities to rearrange the voting by students for their elected officers. As of now on most campuses, the fifty to seventy percent of students who commute to the university know very little about any of the candidates for student office. The residential students, quite often the members of clubs and fraternities and sororities, supply the main organizing for candidates. In this situation it is hard to get a representative cross-section of the student body into office.*

It is equally hard for students to develop a feeling of identity with the university, since they have so little to do with the faculty, the administration, or with other students. They have no sense of belonging to one intellectual and social community. Except for the emotional unity produced by allegiance to football and basketball teams which play in the name of the university, there is nothing with which to identify. There never will be until something is done about the organization of student affairs to put responsibility in student hands and not in the hands of personnel officers representing the administration.

The trouble begins with the present hierarchies, going from boards of trustees to presidents to deans to students on the one hand and to faculty members on the other. The students and the faculty are in this sense both governed

---

* On several campuses, non-resident students have now begun to organize themselves to demand rights, privileges, and facilities they do not at present share with the resident students but for which they are paying through student activities fees. At New York State University in Binghamton, for example, where non-resident students outnumber the residents two to one, the non-residents have built their own organization under the title "Off-Campus College," with student representatives and a student staff which operates from an office in the student center, to which they have given the name "On Campus Off-Campus College Center." They now intend to rent a building to serve as their off-campus center for meetings, study areas, a cooperative store and other projects, and they have plans to buy a bus for taking non-resident students to college events.

by the same governors, but only in the case of the faculty is there any approach to self-government and educational responsibility, and even that can be removed by boards of regents and by acts of state legislatures. When the students denounce the system, as I have said elsewhere, they seldom know what it is, and they usually concentrate their attacks on it through attacking its nearest representative—the university president. Since they are not part of the system except as consumers of its educational products, the students have no direct way of changing it except by attacks on the system as a whole or on its local representatives.

Yet the university president is the symbol of an authority he does not possess. Most of the time it is his responsibility to administer policies made by others—on the one side by boards of control and state legislatures, on the other by faculty committees dealing with internal educational policy. In neither case have the students been involved, and in that sense they are not part of the president's constituency. Therefore, in advance of conflicts and crises, the views of the students are least likely to be taken into account, and after the crises have subsided least likely to be given credit, even when the changes they have been demanding are the ones the university has made.

To add to the ambiguities of the situation, it is now generally assumed that what is needed in the presidential post is a man whose experience fits him for the role of crisis manager, politician, negotiator, and financial executive, which is indeed the case as far as the content of his daily work is concerned. At the same time, it is generally recognized that what the society desperately needs is educational and social leadership from men of intellectual stature and humane principles in the universities who can speak to the concerns of mankind and express truths that can be believed and acted upon. But most boards of control do not want that kind of leadership from the men they appoint, nor do they usually think that presidents in office should make public statements on major issues. Their job is managing the affairs of the university according to trustee policy, and that policy demands that students be kept in their place, which means out of political controversy and out of university policy-making. As a result it is only very rarely that students ever hear bold and compelling statements from their presidents on any of the most important issues now racking American and world society, including the issues of educational change on their own campuses.

This makes it almost impossible for the students to see the president as anything but a manager whose job it is to cope with them, not to educate them. Most presidents never address the student body, and the students they see are the official students who deal with university affairs. Communication between the president and the student body is therefore second or third hand, through student officials, vice presidents for student affairs, the student newspaper, the local press, and television. The student body at large seldom knows the university president either as a person or as a public figure. Since he seldom expresses his own views on public issues or declares his own position on matters of educational philosophy, his capacity for intellectual and educational leadership within the university environment and the American community is reduced to a minimum. He becomes an administrator rather than an educator.

We would do well to examine the case of the experimental college at Franconia, New Hampshire, which, through a series of circumstances, went into bankruptcy two years ago and since then has reconstructed itself through a new educational plan involving community government and an open curriculum. Three students, three faculty members, and three trustees were asked by the trustees to find a new president. Their search ended in the appointment of Leon Botstein, who at the time of his appointment was serving as Assistant to the President of the Board of Education of New York City. Mr. Botstein, who is twenty-three years old, has had research and administrative experience in his Board of Education post, has completed his undergraduate degree at the University of Chicago, and is a candidate for the doctorate degree in history at Harvard.

Under the new Franconia plan, the educational administration is in the hands of four joint committees composed of three students, three faculty members, and three trustees with the president occupying a place on each of the committees. The trustees are working members of the administration rather than absentee supervisors or managers, and are drawn from the ranks of the professions and the community in various fields of education, public service, and community action.

In this plan, the president is directly in touch with all the areas of educational policy and student life, both as an educator and administrator. He has taken part, with his colleagues in the college, in the development of an open curriculum which uses the resources of the student body, the faculty, the trustees, and the community as educational instruments. The curriculum includes community service in the rural areas of New Hampshire—teaching, social welfare, social work, etc.—as well as service in city projects, as part of the students' education. The curriculum is developed on the basis of individual planning by and with the students and is not set within fixed academic limits.

Although the Franconia plan is not immediately transferable from a college with three hundred students in a small rural area of New Hampshire to a university with ten to forty thousand students, the philosophy according to which the college is organized and the president appointed will function well in situations involving mass education. The inclusion of students in equal status with faculty members and trustees in the selection committee for a new president, their inclusion, again in equal status, in the central educational policy-making groups, the function of trustees as colleagues rather than absentee managers, the development of an ongoing rather than a static curriculum—these are all ideas which can and should be transposed into the planning for mass education in the colleges and universities.

When they are so transposed, the president is then chosen for his qualities as an educational colleague who has enough administrative talent to handle the affairs of the institution. He can then work in cooperation with the trustees rather than as their employee. Whenever there are issues affecting relations with the community, student demonstrations, changes in educational policy, or rules for student behavior, there is true representation of all points of view in reaching decisions about action to be taken.

In the long run, unless it is possible to turn the situation around and for the students to join forces with a university in whose affairs they are involved and in whose policies they believe, the doctrine of opposing forces will apply, and the best of the students will be in permanent opposition. As in the case of all politics, the opposition party need not then take responsibility for the welfare and success of its opponents.

The question of course is how to turn the situation around without making the campus a battleground for power struggles between students and the university. It is not merely an article of faith to assume that once the students are given responsibility for self-government and educational policy-making the universities will have an antidote to the recurrence of violence. The strategy of violence and non-negotiable demands by students is only workable for militants when *negotiable* student demands, proposals, and ideas are not fully accepted as legitimate and important contributions to the improvement of the university. When students are in a position to see their ideas taken with the same degree of seriousness as those of the administration and faculty, strong-arm tactics become both unnecessary and undesirable. They interfere not merely with the prerogatives and responsibilities of the faculty and the university as a whole, but with the decisions and policies of the students themselves.

In the case of serious rioting, the national guard would then have had the responsibility of acting as a peacekeeping force, in exactly the same way as the United Nations peacekeeping forces operate in situations like those of the Gaza Strip or Cyprus. The commanders of those forces hold as their basic doctrine that if their troops fire, for whatever reason, on either side of a two-party cease-fire agreement, their mission of peacekeeping has failed. Their concern is with the control of violence and the prevention of harm to persons, not with winning a battle with another armed force.

Another way of saying this is that if the universities concentrate solely on the control of violence rather than on the rearrangement of the authority structure to draw students into the middle of it, the administrators have only their own authority and the backing of the police to impose university rules and policies, with no support from the university community as a whole and the students in particular. Seen from the student side, since the administrators run the university, what happens is their problem, and if it can be solved only by brute force and police action there is something wrong with the way the problem is being handled. The most frightening prospect for the future, if the situation remains unchanged, is the possibility that students, while not encouraging acts of violence by other students, will accept them as a natural consequence of the way the university runs.

I can imagine a situation in a reconstructed scenario for the events at Kent State in which the students who planned the fatal morning demonstration of May fourth would have conferred with the appropriate student or student-faculty public events committee about what they intended to do and about their arrangements for marshals. They would have notified and conferred with university officials and the head of the national guard to confirm the ground rules, which would have included a ban on live ammunition and the role of the guard as a peacekeeping force should the students be unable to control acts of violence by their own members. The students would then have the responsibility of proving by their own actions that the presence of police or guardsmen was both unwarranted and an infringement of the academic freedom of the campus.

To the objection that this sort of procedure is too cumbersome to take account of volatile situations in which demonstrators simply assemble themselves spontaneously and begin trashing the campus as a gesture against all authority, the answer is that once a sensible procedure has been agreed upon and put into effect, those who violate it are acting against the policies of the student body, the faculty *and* the administration, not merely against an authority loosely construed as the "university" or the "system." There might still be trouble, but over a period of time, the trouble would be bound to decrease, since there would be a built-in community attitude and procedure against the use of violence in the university as a way of expressing an educational opinion or changing a national policy.

The point is that if the campus is to be considered a sanctuary that is violated when the police and the national guard are called in to control violence, then uncontrolled or uncontrollable violence is the responsibility of the whole community. If the students as a decision-making part of that community are unwilling or unable to take responsible action to prevent physical harm to themselves or to anyone else, or to prevent the destruction of the campus, they are then faced with the same problem as the administration—how do you prevent people from being assaulted, injured or killed without the presence of some form of law enforcement?

As it is now, the pro-violent minority have no community sanctions against them, some of them are trying themselves out and trying out the university to see how far they can go. If they break windows, burn buildings, take over offices and classrooms, hold faculty members and administrators captive, and then, in a police melee, others are savaged by police officers, the blame shifts from the original acts of violence to the brutality of the police and the collusion of those who called them to the campus.

I start with the proposition that the state police and the national guard have no place on a college campus, and that when they are there, they are automatically committed to the use of their kind of force to establish their kind of order. The next proposition is that if they are to be kept off the campus, the student body, the faculty, and the administration must join together in a unified effort to support the right of assembly for the redress of grievances and to set the rules, principles, and practices according to which those rights can be protected. That includes protection from violence either from inside or outside the campus, with the responsibility for protection put squarely on the shoulders of the leaders of the university community, students, faculty, and administration alike. If they are unable to assure that protection, either through incapacity or through circumstances beyond their control, they are then faced with a joint decision about calling for help from outside. But the time has come to say that if they are to survive the consequences of the use of campus violence, students and universities cannot have it both ways. They either handle the problems themselves, or they are going to have them handled from outside.

5. Some Things to Be Done

In the meantime, there are some minimal things that can be done to change the political tone of the campuses and to move the students into a situation in which they have responsibility, authority, and accountability for what they do. Many of the proposals in the following list are already in effect on some campuses. Although some of them are more applicable to state colleges and public universities than to private ones, the philosophy applies to both.

1. Put the problem of campus violence into perspective by holding a seminar at each University with the policy-making representatives from boards of regents and trustees, administrators, faculty members, and students, using the Final Report of the National Committee on Violence and its eighty-one recommendations for action, plus the Report of the President's Commission on Campus Unrest, as the bases for discussion. If board members or any of the others say that they do not have time to read the documents and attend a seminar, ask them if they think they should go on being members of the board, administration, faculty, or student body, in view of the fact that the future of higher education hangs on what they all do over the next few years.

If at this point in the history of a given institution it is not possible to collect these groups into a seminar, arrange at least two meetings of board members with the faculty, students, and administration to look at the implications of what these two commissions are saying for the development of policy on the local campus. If everything else fails, it is the minimal responsibility of the president of the institution to introduce to his board the ideas of those who have studied the issues of campus violence and dissent—both those on the various commissions and the independent scholars who have been in the middle of the controversies. Otherwise it is quite likely that board members will deal with the issues on the basis of what they read in the papers and what they hear around town and see on television.

The recommendations of the President's Commission on Campus Unrest are clustered around the central theme of reconciliation among all the groups involved in campus troubles, with the leadership toward reconciliation assigned by the Commission to the President of the United States. In this, it seems to me that the Commission is absolutely right, and that there is no point in calling for unity and calm in the universities if government officials go on denouncing students for disagreeing with government policies, and if the governors of states and state legislators insist on installing themselves on the campuses as the managers of educational policy and the arbiters of the exact amount of intellectual freedom to be allowed inside and outside the classrooms.

I would therefore support the full list of recommendations the President's Commission makes for reconciling the conflicts, including the idea of organizing governors' conferences on education in each of the states, and a series of national meetings called by the President to bring together educators, students (black and white), law enforcement officers, governors, and state education officials to make some sensible policies which can be applied nationally. But the reconciliation, if there is to be one, must rest on clear and unequivocal statements about what the university stands for and what the students, faculty members, and administrators have a right to say and do.

There are too many people around the state houses and the back rooms of state politics who see in the issue of controlling the students a wide open chance to bolster their own political records at the expense of freedom in education. There are also too many people inside the universities who incline toward a policy of not stirring up the political animals and of letting them run free through the campuses. When the politicians begin calling on all law-abiding citizens to shut up the long-haired students and their dangerous teachers, that is exactly the time not to seek reconciliation with their point of view but to oppose it vehemently, openly, and without regard to threats about budget-cutting and punishment to the universities.

As was the case in the McCarthy period of the 1950's when the attackers who chose the universities and schools as their targets won most of their victories because the educators did not stand up against them, the present crop of reactionaries led by Mr. Agnew will make further inroads against the freedom of students and teachers in America if the attitude of the universities is to allow them to dictate educational policy in matters which are the true business of educators. It is certainly a time for leadership in reconciliation from the government, but it is even more a time for educators to educate the public in the principles according to which the intellectual life of the country can be protected from its anti-intellectual enemies.

1. In sustaining the philosophy of reconciliation, colleges and universities should elect or appoint to boards of trustees, regents, and controlling bodies in general more students and a more representative cross-section of the American community, from minority groups, the arts, the professions, trade unions, and parents of college students.

2. Install a system of student self-government in which students are asked to take responsibility for legislating on policies in student affairs and for administering their legislation.

3. Establish a small joint committee of students, faculty and administration, to act as an over-all policy committee to which student legislation and policy considered to be unwise by the administration or the faculty, could be referred for decision, the vote of the joint committee being final. Similarly, legislation from the faculty considered by the students or the administration to be unwise could

be brought before the joint committee for discussion and decision.

4. Through the joint committee, draw up a statement of the procedures to be followed by the organizers of public meetings, demonstrations, and rallies which would place the responsibility for the control of possible violence in the hands of the student organizers, through a system of marshals who would meet with the campus security personnel to establish common goals and agreed-upon responsibilities. The statement should include provisions for due process in accordance with the First Amendment and should make clear the grounds for expulsion or suspension.

5. Make clear in written policy statements the fact that criminal acts punishable by law are a matter between those who commit the crimes and the law enforcement agencies, and that the universities cannot, even if they wanted to, intervene in providing sanctuary.

6. Assure the students through written policy statements that university records containing personal or political material about individuals in the student body or faculty will not be released to investigating or police agencies.

7. Revise student election procedures to ensure that the student governing bodies are fully representative of the university as a whole. Minority groups at present unrepresented or under-represented could be invited to elect their own representatives as an interim step; other student groups within the campus community could be invited to send observers and non-voting representatives to meetings of the student governing bodies.

8. Appoint a committee of trustees to meet regularly on the campus with the students responsible for student self-government in a continuing seminar on education and student affairs.

9. Establish liaison of a similar kind between students and members of the education and budget committees of

the state legislature so that when issues of campus unrest
are raised publicly, both the students and the state legislators have direct information on the point of view and
actions of each.

10. Hold open student meetings on the campuses to discuss political and social issues with representatives from
boards of trustees, the administration, the legislature,
alumni, the faculty, and the student body.

11. Organize student campaigns for the election of
students and faculty members to the state legislature
and municipal governments, and encourage students to
work with other candidates and legislators as speech-
writers, research assistants, and campaign organizers.

12. Include students as voting members of all major
university committees, and provide ways in which they
can be included in the process of making major university
appointments, including the appointment of the president
and tenured professors.

13. Establish a regular time for the president to meet
with students, to provide ways in which he can have a
direct relation with the student body at large; for example, through bi-weekly open briefing sessions at which
he agrees to speak, to present other members of his administration on specific points, and to answer questions.

14. Since the main, and sometimes the only, relationship of the students with the university is through their
attendance at classes, use class time in some sort of informal or regular way for the discussion of issues in
educational policy as they affect the lives of the students,
with the faculty members taking responsibility for informing themselves on the issues and inviting students
to prepare brief position papers and presentations.

15. Use the resources of the faculty, through the departments, to form student-faculty study groups within
some of the existing courses to work on university problems—the political rights of students, the relation of education to politics, financial aid to students, educational

reform, etc.—so that the ongoing work of the courses feeds ideas and research into the main stream of educational discussion. This would include studies done through the courses on issues raised by student unrest at the time the issues are being raised. The subject of student unrest itself could be a matter for research and study by students in the courses as well as for graduate student theses.

16. Encourage experiments in student-initiated courses and research programs that are directly related to the work of student government so that the gap between what goes on in the academic curriculum and the concerns of the students is at least partially closed.

17. Make available the basic figures for the university budget to the students, and invite the appropriate student representatives to form an advisory committee on university finance. More often than not, student criticisms of university spending are based on inadequate information about the financial situation, especially in the private colleges. Students should know where the money comes from and where it goes.

18. Since parents occupy the role of interested parties, both in their children's education and in university policy as it affects the public, organize parents' committees for the purpose of informing parents in general about educational policies. Hold occasional university meetings planned by a student-parent-faculty committee, with speakers from each group and discussion of local and national educational issues.

19. Above all, concentrate on the improvement of the quality of university teaching and student learning. The heart of the university lies in its teaching program, and until students are absorbed in an intellectual life that is exciting, vigorous, and rewarding, they are not going to be able to commit themselves to the values of the university as an intellectual center or to make those values a central part of the lives they lead when they leave the campus.

Some of these suggestions are versions or extensions of what is already being done at many universities; others go farther than many of the universities are as yet ready to go. None of the suggestions is particularly radical, although taken together they can have a serious effect in changing the climate of the campuses to one in which students are willing and able to take responsibility for their own university.

6. How Changes Come About

Another way of looking at these or any other proposals for change in education is to ask how changes have actually come about in the past and how they can be brought about in the present. The most immediate answer is that changes inside the educational system have come primarily from outside. The society and the goals it has set for itself exert the pressures, assert the demands, and supply the funds for doing what the society wants done.

One of the best recent examples is the Sputnik syndrome, whose main effect in educational change came from political competition in space science with the Soviet Union. Curricular changes in the direction of stiffening academic requirements and revising the science curriculum were made with a pace approaching the speed of light once the necessity of the competition was established in the public mind and in the mind of government, foundation and educational executives. The teachers and their new curricula were rushed along by the social and political system, not by the internal forces or creative imagination of the educational system itself.

The leadership in the movement toward the reforms in science teaching came from a variety of sources outside, ranging from Admiral Rickover's criticisms and proposals, Professor Zacharias' writing and experimental work, Senator Benton's comparisons of Soviet educational strength with what were said to be our weaknesses, to the ideas of James Conant and others: all of these men occupied positions of strength in the government and foundation establishment. The movement for change went from the public expression in the mass media of a body of ideas by prestigious public figures into the places where money in large quantity could be had and where the social

and educational controls were centered. From there it
went into the schools and colleges where the changes pre-
viously worked out by university professors on foundation
and government grants were put into effect by the administrators with the cooperation of teachers and textbook publishers. The changes did not come from the educators' or the teachers' initiative.

In the past five years, another set of political and social
forces has been at work, having to do with race relations,
the war, social disorder and the problems of poverty. The
pressure of these forces has brought about changes in
educational thinking; the student movement itself is part
of the general movement for change produced in the
middle of a complex of political, social, and economic fac-
tors. Just as President Kennedy stated the basic political
doctrine of space competition with the Soviets in the early
1960's, so President Johnson set the next doctrine from
1964 until 1968 with the war on poverty and the war in
Vietnam mixed together as contradictory national goals.
Then the social legislation of the Eighty-eighth and
Eighty-ninth Congresses put new changes in motion.
These included the rise in expectations of the poor and
the blacks and led to increased militancy and initiative
by all the under-classes, along with the resistance of the
students to being used as cannon fodder and manpower
for government aims, and the rise of new national leaders
with their own kind of prestige and influence—Martin
Luther King, Malcolm X, Eldridge Cleaver, Robert Kennedy, and others. All of this helped to create the political
and social context in which changes in education were
again forced upon the educators.

This is not to say that the impact of educational ideas
from educators, intellectuals and proponents of radical
change within the academic profession were not a factor.
They were, but for the most part they came from writers
outside the educational system, and the spread of their

ideas was only possible because of the change in the political context in which they wrote. Aside from Clark Kerr, the last major figure among the university presidents to have serious national influence on university policy was James Conant, whose base of operation was Harvard but whose connections to the power structure extended to the Washington agencies and to the national policy-makers within the major foundations. For some of the reasons already set down, university presidents have in the last ten years had a diminishing influence on educational policy, both nationally and within their own institutions. The actual process of internal change has been in the hands of the faculty and the students, and it is the students who have been taking the major initiatives.

As a result, in the crisis of student revolt, the major policy statements on educational change are still coming from outside, where the power is, from Governor Reagan, President Nixon, John Gardner, state and government commissions, and boards of regents, with the university presidents placed in the role of mere advisers to the government on policy rather than as educational leaders in their own communities and in American social change. Inside the universities, the main source of power for administrators in making reforms lies in their decisions on the allocation of the budget, their power of appointment of other administrators, and their relation to the faculty and students.

The two examples of administrative success I have already cited, Yale and Princeton, are both of universities where the president has a relationship of mutual respect with the internal community of students and faculty, based on a readiness to listen and to take the student seriously, a decent regard for the prerogatives and responsibilities of the faculty, and a body of ideas on social and educational change that shows intelligent so-

cial concern. The administrators and their colleagues
among the students and faculty can therefore get things
done by working together.

In other institutions it is often true that the president,
vice presidents and deans are much more open to reform
in the educational program than are the faculty. Alliances can be made between the students and the administration for projects and changes that do not have to wait
for faculty approval since they can be organized without
permission, inside the existing system.

A president also has the nerve-racking duty of worry-
ing about the financial problems of his institution, a duty
which can very well take up all his time, with trips to
Washington, around the alumni circuit, dinners for private donors, meetings with his fund-raisers, and speeches
to dozens of community groups. If there is one problem
for the university president that dwarfs all others, it is
the problem of finance, especially, but not exclusively,
in the private colleges and universities. In the case of
the private universities, we have reached a point where
there is simply not enough money to be had through private giving and foundation grants to make up the enormous deficits that are increasing annually, and there is a
finite limit to the amount of tuition that *can* be charged,
aside from the question of whether it should be charged
at all.

Nevertheless, the money that is actually in the budget
is allocated from the administrative offices, and in the
case of administrators who have creative ideas for change
and are in touch with their students, faculty, and sources
of funds, projects may be started that can in the long run
have profound effects in changing educational policy.
What the administrators cannot do is to change the system itself either by placing revisionist plans before the
faculty or by taking administrative action of their own.
They can help others to change what they want to change,

they can persuade by force of reason in informal talks and formal meetings, but the system is one they have inherited and cannot overthrow.

As of now, one of the reasons for the slow rate of university change, aside from the institutional inertia built into the present structure, is that not much is understood in the faculty and student body about how changes can best be brought about. Most efforts to find out are defeated by the fact that any broad institutional change must have a consensus of faculty approval, and everything must go through the elaborate system of faculty committees and study groups on its way to the collective faculty body. In my visits to campuses I have often found myself within a period of two to three days talking with at least six to eight committees, usually student-faculty groups, although sometimes separately organized. In almost every case the method of change adopted has been the preparation of committee reports with recommendations but no power, submitted to the faculty and administration for action.

Sometimes that works, most of the time it does not. The reports themselves are usually conservative documents, written in the political context of the internal affairs of the university with one eye on the departments and the other on the administration and board of control. Admonitions are continually given that this idea or that one is very good and very important but it would not get by a faculty vote, or it would not get by the administration, or it would cost too much. The result is that the affliction of the watered-down report prevents the possibility of serious proposals for serious change, and may even prevent discussion of the real issues in favor of some form of simple rearrangement of credits or requirements or student-faculty relations.

The most celebrated example of the failure of the committee report may serve as a warning to universities in their search for reform. It comes from the Muscatine

Report at the University of California at Berkeley, prepared in the aftermath of the Free Speech Movement in 1964 and 1965. It is an impressive document that sums up the thinking of a faculty committee drawn from all parts of the university, with forty-two recommendations for reform based on an extensive analysis of the system of instruction and its faults.

In a review of the effect of the report since it was first introduced to the Berkeley faculty and administration, Martin Trow points out that the reason it was so widely acclaimed initially was that it has "the virtue of not affecting anybody who does not want to be affected by it. . . . If the Report is notable for the lack of dispute it has occasioned, it is largely because virtually all of its many recommendations can be ignored by those who are simply not interested." *

Among other methods of change, the most dramatic is of course student protest and revolt, with demands backed up by boycotts, strikes, sit-ins, takeovers. Some of the Black Studies and other programs were introduced in a very short time by that method. The method does produce change in a hurry, but leaves a great deal to be desired as a long-term policy. Whatever else a long-term policy should contain, experience has shown that it will have to work out a way of including the students centrally in its formation.

Here then is the dilemma. Those of us who argue for radical reform as a necessity for saving the colleges and universities have to face the fact that except in the special case of the experimental colleges and a handful of those that have recently been designed at the outset as experimental institutions, radical reform of American higher

* Martin Trow, "Bell, Book and Berkeley: Reflections Occasioned by a Reading of Daniel Bell's *The Reforming of General Education.*" *Experiment and Innovation*, vol. 1 (January, 1968), p. 9, quoted by Joseph Fashing, unpublished Ph.D. dissertation, University of Oregon, December 1969.

education on a system-wide basis is impossible by present methods other than those of militant student activism. Yet if the radical reforms are not made, there is no doubt that the activism will increase in its militancy, and university disruptions followed by ad hoc changes will continue to be the method of making educational policy.

For these reasons and others, it seems to me that we should take the reforms straight to the center of where the education is being carried on—in the present classes —and without waiting for university-wide changes in policy, concentrate on direct and immediate collaboration between students and faculty members, with the help of the administration, in making changes in teaching styles and curriculum in the courses now being taught. While the long-range plans are being made for the reform of university government and the general reform of the system, there are specific things that can be done in the immediate present wherever there are individuals and groups among the faculty and students who want to work together inside or outside the system.

When you look for the place where the primary relation between the student and his education now exists, you find it in his courses and his classes. It should obviously move out from there into wider areas of experience, but in the meantime that is where it is. What is missing is an educational instrument through which the changes which students and teachers agree are desirable and necessary can be put into effect right away and legitimized on a university-wide basis without struggling with the cumbersome machinery of institutional change as it slowly grinds its way into the future.

I urge the strategy of the amoeba, with many projects everywhere, creating more projects everywhere else, until there is evolution into a different organism. There are many different kinds of centers for such growth, but the one which I choose as the best available model is a combination of the ideas behind the student experimental

college, the free school, and free university movement,
and the more conventional student-faculty committee on
educational development, in this case converted into a
center for planning rather than remaining a judicial body
to decide what courses may be offered for credit. There
are ways of linking such a central agency to every other
part of the student and faculty community, through action research, course planning, inter-departmental collaboration, student government, and simple invitations to
join the movement. The aim of the student-faculty educational development committee, institute, or whatever it
might be called, would be to create new open experimental
programs, partly inside and partly outside the present
system, in which all ideas for change and innovation have
a free chance to be tested. Those which turn out well and
establish themselves through experiment as useful, rewarding, and intellectually important can move from
there into the continuing parts of the university teaching
program.

Had there been such a student-faculty body with free
access to students with educational ideas and programs,
many of the confrontations and non-negotiable demands
of the Black Studies advocates would have been avoided,
along with a great deal of the separatism which accom-
panied the movement for a new black curriculum. The
danger of segregating Black Studies into its own institutes and institutional forms and treating the introduction of new materials into the curriculum as a problem of
combining them all in single units is that the curriculum
change is too slight. What should be the saturation of the
entire social sciences and humanities curriculum with
new ideas for content drawn from a broad base of historical, social, political, and psychological concepts is
limited to a specific body of material dealt with in a single
section of the university.

The case of introducing new material from non-Western cultures into the curriculum by forming area studies programs and non-Western courses is typical: the effect is to make up another area of subject matter rather than infusing the educational system with a wealth of new thinking about all cultures and all varieties of human life. The psychology offerings, for example, should deal with a wide range of new material in the comparative study of human growth and development, with special attention to the American minorities. It is just as important to do new work in this field as it is to add new courses in Afro-American or Spanish-American history to the offerings of the history department. What the university needs is an operating center for educational change right at the heart of its curriculum planning. Otherwise there is no place for good ideas to go except through the frustrating committee system.

A warning about what not to do to organize this kind of change agency comes from the experience at Berkeley, where a faculty Board of Educational Development, recommended by the Muscatine Report, turned into a judicial board to allow or disallow student-initiated courses to be granted credit, while the students had organized a Center for Participant Education as a means of developing new courses and programs which could be presented to the Board as university offerings. It was not long before the two groups had fallen into an adversary relationship, as they were bound to in view of the local situation and the separation of students into proposers and the faculty into judges. The relationship was worsened by the double circumstance of faculty inertia and disinterest along with interference by the board of regents and the administration.

But the basic idea remains sound, and in various forms in other institutions has proven to be useful. It needs to be strengthened and expanded. In essence it consists of making a central operating agency in the student body for creative thought and action in educational change,

and linking it to the working parts of policy-making in
the university as a whole. It does not preempt other
methods and programs of change, but it does give the
idea of change a place in which it can live and grow, and
if that place is recognized by the faculty and administration as a central part of the university structure, it can
do more than any other single agency to keep the university open to new educational ideas.

The success of one of the variations of the Student
Center for Educational Reform or the free university
rests ultimately on the degree of interest and support it
gains from the students. But it must also depend, for the
development of its ideas and its growth in influence, on
the faculty and the administration. There is a delicate
balance to be established between cooperation by the faculty and the initiative of the students, otherwise the idea
falls back into the regular faculty curriculum committee
arrangement by which all decisions are in the hands of
the faculty. There is no reason why ideas cannot flow
from the faculty to the students in their center for reform, once the concept of educational change is accepted
as something important enough for everybody to do something about. With a student leadership that changes
every year and the natural shift of interest in the student
body from one issue to another, a continuing flow of initiative and support from the faculty as well as from the
students is essential to the continuity of the change.

In a student body of ten to fifteen thousand, in most
cases not more than one hundred to five hundred students
become directly involved in student affairs of any kind.
When meetings on educational issues are held, unless
there has been some sort of dramatic confrontation or
serious trouble, not more than one to three hundred students attend. There are many explanations for this, including the fact that a large percentage of the students
at state colleges and universities, especially in the urban
areas, hold jobs, and that a large percentage are com-

muters and are simply not on the campus enough to become involved in university affairs; the same thing is true of the faculty. But the main reason is that the system, as it now works, consists almost entirely of class attendance for which credit is given, and there is no particular reason why a student should involve himself in university affairs since it is in no sense his responsibility. Attendance at classes is the only thing that is required or requested of him and of his teachers.

That fact came clear in a startling way, to the disappointment of many faculty members, at the time of the May 1970 student strike. On many campuses, once the initial rallies, demonstrations, and meetings were over in the first few days, and once arrangements had been made for cancelling examinations, awarding credit, and the rest in order to allow for work on the issues before the country, the student body simply disappeared. Since there were no classes, there was no obligation to do anything else unless one were a member of the minority that was deeply involved in the issues themselves.

Among some faculty members and administrators, this was considered another proof that students are irresponsible and uninterested in either the cause of peace and justice or in their own education. Their conduct was interpreted as simply wanting to avoid the trouble of taking examinations and spending another two weeks being educated. It is perfectly true that once the props were removed from the system, there was nothing but the student's own interest to keep him on the campus. But to me, this is a sign of the failure of the system as it works, not of a failure in the students. They have been taught that education is going to class and adding up credits. Once there are no classes, there is no point in trying to learn any other way, since going to class is the only thing that counts on the record.

7. What Is Wrong

What is wrong with the university as a teaching institution is precisely this: It has no philosophy of education, no unifying principle around which reforms can be made, either to meet the problems of student unrest or to engage the students in their own learning.

It has instead a system of administrative conveniences. The whole apparatus of departments, divisions, institutes, lectures, research, grades, examinations, academic credits, classes, and faculty appointments is based on an administrative plan for dealing with students and academic subject matter, not on a philosophy.

But how can thirty thousand students, fifteen hundred faculty members, sixty-seven buildings, sixty to seventy administrators, a string of parking lots, a president and ten to twenty regents all have a philosophy of education, or a philosophy of anything? There is no compulsion on either the student or the teacher to submit to a philosophical test before being allowed to join the university, nor, beyond the general statements in the university catalogue is there any public recognition by the university that it functions according to a set of philosophical and psychological principles.

Where can a philosophy come from? Who has it? Is it in the mind of the president who then administers it to the rest? Is it in the collective faculty body, which seldom meets except in crisis, among whom the philosophers themselves have only that kind of philosophy which keeps them studying sentences and trying to get the fly out of the bottle? Or in the students, that mixture of educational products of the American high school who happen to be at a given university at a given time because there is nowhere else to go? Is it in the textbooks of the education courses?

It is in none of these places, and there is not even a rationale that educators agree on for what is now being done in the name of higher education. The point is that the social philosophy and the philosophy of education according to which the system of higher education operates is not explicit, aside from the accepted generalizations about equality of opportunity for all, the need for standards of educational quality, the idea of a community of scholars, academic freedom, or the three-fold functions of research, teaching, and public service. The philosophy is implicit in the system, and to discover what the philosophy is you have to look at the way the system works and the effects it has on the students and the faculty.

If you look at the lecture system, for example, you find that it is based on certain philosophical and psychological assumptions, unstated but deeply fallacious. It assumes that all learning and thinking is conscious, and that the mind is as Locke described it—a clean slate on which sense impressions and ideas are written. It assumes an old-fashioned, pre-Freudian dualism in which the mind is separated from the body, the emotions from the intellect, the conscious from the unconscious. In spite of everything we now know about communication, about symbols, signs, words, images, memory, intuition, and the way ideas and values are communicated from one person to another or from the world to the people in it, it assumes that the best way to communicate ideas and facts is to sit people down in chairs in large groups and talk at them. Even a cursory look at the system shows how shallow and fallacious is the philosophy on which it rests.

Yet it goes on and on, sanctified by custom and convenience. The system is what it is, not by imaginative educational thinking and the continual search for alternatives, but by the gradual accretion over the years of such practices as seemed administratively useful at the time they were installed. That is how the lecture system began and was frozen into the structure before books and other learning instruments were invented, and why it now continues unchecked. It is the simplest way of handling classes of fifty to one thousand students, and as more students come to the colleges and universities, they are simply added to the existing classes, since it does not matter how many people sit down together to listen to the same lecturer. They are all intended to hear the same thing at the same time, and it is just a question of finding a room big enough to hold them, or a closed circuit television system to reach them in smaller rooms.

The same doctrine is true for the academic credit, testing and grading system that is interlocked with the lectures. They all go together. The credit idea was first introduced to make it easier for students to transfer from one university to another, and the units of credit along with the grades could tell the registrar at one institution about where the student fitted into the program at another. The idea spread from there, where it had a limited usefulness, until it has corrupted the entire system of education from elementary school to graduate study. There is no good educational reason for keeping track of students that way, and there is every reason to show how intellectually and psychologically naive it is to count up an education in hours, courses, and fragments of time spent in one-dimensional learning.

In any case, when students and other contemporary critics condemn the system they are not arguing philosophical or psychological principles. They are saying that it is bad education and that its practical effect is to dull their interest in learning and frustrate their efforts to become educated. If you look at the system as it now works it is not very hard to see why, nor is it hard to see what the changes are that must be made once the university is redefined as a place for students to learn what they need to know in order to be fully human. In what follows I have put together a preliminary list of changes to be made, along with the reasons for making them. Although they do express a philosophy of education which could be described as a body of ideas, I am not arguing for the

changes on philosophical grounds at the moment. They
are simply practical things to be done for the improvement of education, things that I know will work because
I have seen their results when they have been put into
practice.

I am not arguing that if these changes were made, we
would immediately have an instant cure for student unrest, the disruptions of the campuses, the disorders in the
society, and the malaise of twentieth-century man. But I
do say that it seems to me to be odd that in all the recent
concern shown by government commissions and educational study groups with the existence of student unrest
it seems not to have occurred to the educators to see what
could be done by the simple device of taking the education of students in all the dimensions of their need—political, aesthetic, intellectual, social, and personal—with
a seriousness at least equal to theirs.

One of the reasons for that lack is that their education
is, in fact, *given* to them. It is administered to them under
certain conditions not of their own making; they don't do
it themselves. When they break away from the regular
pattern of university courses and make their own programs with the help of their teachers and others, as they
have in the free university and student experimental college movement, they choose to work seriously on matters
of importance to them, to their society and to their own
state of mind. The attitude of the university community
is then transformed from one of protest into intellectual
activism, involvement, and for a period of time, even ex-
hilaration.

Leave aside for the moment whether or not all the subjects for discussion, and all the interests in which students then indulge are of lasting importance, to them or
to the history of knowledge. Grant that some of the topics
they include in the ad hoc curriculum are fashionable and
pass from campus to campus like habits of dress. The
single most important fact about this kind of intellectual

breakout is that it raises the level of intellectual effort
and broadens the areas of intellectual and social concern,
surely two of the major purposes of any serious educational institution.

Leave aside too the difficulties in sustaining that level
of interest over an extended period—a semester or a year
—and the problem of putting together sequential studies
such as those needed in some branches of the natural
sciences, or in studies in depth of the issues first raised by
the students. Suppose you do get an improvised student
curriculum that runs out of material after a month. This
kind of experience of organizing a curriculum is important in its own right. It teaches students how to run their
own education, and for one thing, teaches them how hard
that is. The problems of sustained sequential studies are
often impossible to solve by the students themselves. But
they can be solved when their teachers begin to work with
them and add the dimensions of their own knowledge, interest and understanding to the enterprises the students
have already begun.

The activist students continually make the argument
that in the present system they are being put through a
particular set of courses the society and its universities
have decided will prepare them to fit into the present social and economic order, that they are given the official
culture, the official line. They are right. That is what they
are given, and it is another reason for their restlessness.

Students have discovered some things about their society for themselves and they want to go on discovering
more. They have developed a kind of Naderism throughout the whole of the student movement—a look at all
courses and programs with a sceptical eye and an interest
in testing the claims made by educators for the educational models they are putting out year after year. The
students in the professional schools have been looking at
what is given to them and have noticed the absence of law
for the poor in the law schools, medicine for the poor in

the medical schools, the lack of the creative arts in the humanities division, and any number of other gaps and handicaps. They are going to go on questioning all the forms of education offered to them, and they are going to develop more of their own forms as they become more experienced in planning student projects. There is no reason why the university cannot take full advantage of this supply of educational talent in the student body, not merely as a way of curing unrest but as a way of raising the level of commitment of all students to an understanding of the issues and ideas that affect mankind. That is the main point. The educational problem is not with the minority of protesters and activists who are raising the basic questions and insisting on basic changes. It is with the eighty to ninety percent of those who accept the system as they find it, and, in the absence of teaching which can arouse their intellectual and moral commitments, remain in a state of mental and social acquiescence.

Here then is a list of what the activist students say is wrong with their education in the university. The list is not drawn from the radical literature or the action programs of the militants, although most of them would agree with it. It is a summary of what most concerned students say on the basis of their own experience.

What Is Wrong With the University According to the Students

1. The university has remained aloof from the moral, political and social issues of contemporary society and has simply acted as the servant of the status quo, selling its services to the highest bidder and ignoring the true interest and needs of the students and the American people.
2. Students have no real part in making educational and social policy and are being programmed by others to fit into an unjust, undemocratic, and racist society.
3. Faculty members, who control the curriculum and the teaching system, are concerned with following their own academic careers and not with the education of students.
4. The teaching has therefore been of low quality, de-

humanized, mechanized, and organized in a system made
to suit the convenience of the faculty.

5.   The system consists of:

(a) Professors lecturing to students in large classes three
times a week, in fifty-minute periods, with one period a
week for discussion sections and tests. Most of the lectures are boring and cover ground also covered in assigned textbooks written by other professors who are
also boring.

(b) Students taking required courses, either as general
requirements for the B.A. degree or as special requirements of the subject matter departments, with few other
options. The student is locked into whatever courses the
faculty decides he must take, and no matter how bad
the course and the teacher, the student has no escape and
has little chance to plan his own education. This results
in low motivation, or at the very least, no encouragement
for developing a motivation on the part of those who are
already unmotivated.

(c) Five courses are to be taken as the regular number
each semester in order to graduate in four years, with
three units of academic credit for each course. This
fragments the student's time and makes it impossible
for him to do justice to any one subject, since with
fifteen classes a week plus the discussion and test sections, with each class taught in the same way by lectures
and reading assignments, there is no time left to think
about what is being learned, and not enough is taught
about any one thing.

(d) An examination and grading apparatus which is
used to measure and award credit for the way in which
the student meets the expectations of the teacher. This
means that the student is constantly and anxiously
working to make a good grade rather than learning the
subject, while the examinations, sometimes in the form
of objective tests administered bi-weekly, measure what
he has remembered rather than what he is capable of
doing as a thinking person.

(e) Departmental majors by which the student must
take courses in the junior and senior year which are
geared to the academic requirements of graduate school
rather than to the development of the student's interests
and intellectual ability.

6.   The total effect of this system is therefore to divorce
learning from life, to put the student in a passive role,
and to force him through the study of materials which
are irrelevant to his own interests and to the needs and
problems of the society around him.

7.   Both the curriculum and the admissions policies are

stacked in favor of white middle-income students from
suburban or urban high schools where from eighty to
ninety-five percent of all seniors go on to college. This
means that when intelligent students whose academic
preparation has been poor are admitted to college, they
find it very hard to keep up in a competitive system which
puts its primary emphasis on the skills of academic learning, and in a high proportion of cases are flunked out or
drop out through discouragement.

8.   The political and social pressures on the students and
faculty in the public universities from boards of regents
and state legislatures are so great that student and faculty activism is repressed, academic freedom is stifled,
and campus dissent is met by police action, tear gas, clubs,
and guns.

9.   The social restrictions of campus life treat the student
as a child rather than as a responsible young adult, and
prevent him from enjoying the ordinary privileges of pri-
vacy and freedom which he would have if he were not in
college.

10.   University presidents and administrative officers are
crisis managers, fund-raisers, politicians, and bureau-
crats, not educators, and they have little knowledge of student realities and little respect for student opinion unless
it coincides with their own or unless they are forced to
pay attention to students and their views through student
confrontations. Since they are responsible to the conservative boards of trustees that appoint them to office, to
alumni, to potential donors, and to state legislative bodies,
and they are hired to carry out board policy, they seldom
take stands on any political or social issues, and are face-
less office-holders rather than cultural and educational
leaders. They therefore have little influence on student
opinion or on the quality of the students' education.

Other items could be added to the list, and a fair percentage of faculty members and administrators could
be added as voluntary witnesses to its accuracy. I agree
with the analysis. The analysis implies change, and I propose a series of changes, the reasons for making them,
and some suggestions about how they might be made.
They are proposals intended to be practical; that is, they
can be acted upon without increases in budgets, foundation grants, major upheavals, or abrupt departures from
everything that is now done.

In saying this, I do not wish to seem to be against major upheavals and abrupt departures or to lose my franchise as an advocate of radical education. I simply accept the fact that the upheavals and abrupt departures are already going on, by other means, and I am looking for ways of making the departures permanent. Some of the changes suggested are already under way in some institutions, others have not yet begun. Most of them apply more directly to the four years of undergraduate work in the arts and sciences than to the professional and graduate schools, although the philosophy of change remains the same in both cases. The professional schools are equally in need of overhauling and some of them are getting it.

I begin with the question of academic requirements.

8. Whose Body of Knowledge?

Remove All Subject Matter Requirements for Graduation and Arrange Instead for Each Student to Choose His Own Teachers and Courses and to Plan a Year to Year Curriculum of His Own.

The reason for removing the requirements is not to make things easier for the student by allowing him to avoid "hard" courses. It is to get him directly involved in his own education and to make the faculty members more responsible to students for the quality and content of the teaching they have to offer. No matter how many students are assembled together on a campus, each of them is a single person, alone within himself, and it is the single person who is ultimately to be educated by whatever means are adopted. Since each person is different, and each person is different from himself at different times in his life, not all students can be educated, or can be expected to respond, in exactly the same way at the same time. Nor is there one body of knowledge which all men must have in order to fulfill themselves in their capacities, nor is there a necessary order in which everything should be learned. There are different capacities, fed by different kinds of intellectual and cultural nourishment at different times throughout a life. One thing leads to another.*

The undergraduate years are a time for creating new interests, not just for channeling them, a place for beginning the exploration of the mind and the world, not for ending it. Once the interests are deeply held and firmly fixed, including the interest in learning, they will con-

---

* The case for a free curriculum is argued at some length in Harold Taylor, *Students Without Teachers: The Crisis in the University* (New York: McGraw-Hill, 1969), Chapters 8, 9, 11, and 12.

tinue into life after college, and what is not learned there
in one year or in four can be learned elsewhere and later
on, at any given point when the need arises.

Another reason for freeing the student from requirements is that no one learns anything seriously and well
unless he commits himself to it, sees the reason for it,
and has a stake in what he is learning. This is commonly
recognized in most other parts of life, it is ignored only
in the educational institutions. If your stake is merely to
get rid of a college requirement, as is usually the case
among students, you are unlikely to learn very much of
lasting importance, although naturally, any course of
study which is beautifully taught is worth taking for its
own sake.

If a student wants to be a physicist, or a dancer, a so-
ciologist or a doctor, certain kinds of courses and teachers
will obviously have to be chosen; the absence of requirements does not mean that physicists should not study
physics because courses in that subject are not required.
For the proposal is not simply to abolish requirements
and leave everything lying around loose in a new kind of
laissez-faire. It is to clear the way for a new system of
learning in which responsibility for choice and commitment is put where it belongs—in the hands of the learner.
He is then made accountable, to himself and to his teachers, for what he does with his education.

As new goals and new interests arise, and they will if
the system works properly, they impose their own requirements, and the student must choose the courses of
study and kinds of activities which lead to the fulfillment
of the goals he has set for himself. He chooses his way
toward becoming the kind of person the education he
chooses will make it possible for him to be. The act of
choosing makes it necessary for him to decide on his purposes. That is one of the things that is missing in the
present system. There is very little in it to evoke in the

student a sense of purpose other than the general aim of getting through the courses in the least amount of time with the highest possible grade.

Although the number of requirements for graduation varies from college to college, the usual pattern involves two years of general education in the arts and sciences followed by another set of departmental requirements for a major in a given field, plus whatever additional requirements there are for graduate school. There is no evidence that I have found convincing to prove that students become broadly or liberally educated by taking general education courses. What usually happens is that the students skim the surface of the conventional wisdom in a given academic field, treat the courses as a duty to be done, and gain a false idea of what it means to be liberally educated.

As for the necessity of deciding on a "major" and fulfilling its requirements, this seems to me to be one of the more pernicious elements in the present system, since it forces the student to choose a field of academic study designed to produce candidates for the graduate schools rather than educated men and women. The purpose of undergraduate education is to encourage intellectual exploration, to help the student put together a body of knowledge which is genuinely his own. There is little chance for him to do that if his main educational assignment is to master the content of someone else's curriculum.

Nor have I seen evidence to convince me that the standard pre-medical or pre-law or pre-anything course sequences are either a necessary or desirable preparation for work in a professional school later on. Certainly there are areas of study appropriate to the student who intends to become a lawyer, a doctor, or an architect, but precisely what these are cannot be determined by an over-all decision about a standard body of subject matter for everyone. When the student is asked to take a direct part in designing his own education he will inevitably have to take account of what he intends to use his education for. But this does not mean that he must sacrifice range and depth in his intellectual and personal development in order to become a professional in a given field.

In an open curriculum students need more help in putting together a program of studies for themselves than they can get under the present system. In the present system, the faculty adviser or the student personnel office simply tells you what the requirements are, what you have to do to meet them, how much of this and how much of that, and, occasionally, if he is a gifted adviser, how to get around the system.

Without the crutch of the requirements, the student is in a situation in which there is pressure on him to take his choices seriously. Discussions of courses and teachers then involve many more questions than are ordinarily raised under the advising system now in operation. Some of it will be at the simple level of asking how good a given teacher is, what kind of course he teaches, what has been the experience of other students in it, what sort of marking system the teacher uses, how much work is expected, what sort of reading assignments, how often the classes meet, and so on.

But even this will demand that each teacher be much more explicit about what he intends doing in his course. He will need to describe it in writing, and he will need to find ways of conferring with students about his work, both the students who have already been working with him and those who are trying to decide whether to or not. He will also be more interested in making certain that the advising system works in such a way that it conveys accurate statements to the student body about the character and style of his courses and the place they occupy in the curriculum in general.

Under the present system, there is no built-in way in which the pressure of student opinion and judgment can improve the quality of teaching and the content of courses, since the faculty is protected from desertion by students through the simple device of the requirements for graduation. Even if you know that a course is useless and badly taught there is not very much you can do about it if you have to take it to graduate. Removal of the requirements forces each teacher to reconsider any number of questions about his own teaching, and in the best of situations, he is naturally drawn toward cooperation with his students in working out the style and content of the learning they are to do together.

It also means a great deal more freedom for the teacher to develop new courses of his own which represent more truly than is now the case what he has to offer to the education of the student body. Most of the requirements for the departmental and general education courses are built on a standardized syllabus which teachers are required to teach, and the students required to learn. As of now, most of the introductory and intermediate courses are locked to each other in sequence, and the student is told that he cannot take the second one without the first. This not only has a negative effect on the brilliant young teacher who is saddled with someone else's ideas about what and how he should be teaching, but it has no positive effect in raising the level of the average teacher who can float along with the syllabus indefinitely, without an educational thought in his head, and can always say to his student critics that it is not his fault that the course isn't working, he has to teach it that way because it is required.

Since the student in an open curriculum is bound to be asking more questions about what he will study and how this fits his own interests and intentions, he will need people to talk to who are fairly sophisticated and intelligent about the university and its teachers and programs,

about what to do with his life and talent, his weaknesses
and strengths, or about anything else that comes up in
the normal course of going to college and living in the
1970's. One of the troubles with the present system is that
in it most students never raise such questions on their own,
and nobody in the university raises them either. The
guidance and faculty advising programs in most universities are educationally useless, for some of the reasons
I have already given. Most faculty members want nothing
to do with them, they take up office time, and the students,
unless they are already highly motivated, don't want to
spend *their* time talking about matters which are already
settled by the regulations of the dean's office.

Whatever good advising there now is usually comes to
students from other students; and, although the advice
varies in quality from the cynicism of seniors about doing
anything at all, to the explicit and mature comments of
the educational activists, it is basically sound advice because it comes from the lived-through experience of educational practitioners who see the system from the inside.
What they see is usually depressing and the advice they
give is of the kind published by the Berkeley students
beginning in 1965—how to get an education in spite of
the system.

On the other hand, with the sharply increased interest
of more and more students in reforming the institutions
they attend, some of the best educational writing being
done is by students, addressed to other students. It comes
in the form of reports on courses and teachers, studies of
the grading system, proposals for reform, editorials, and
articles in the over-ground and underground student
press, bulletins from the Educational Reform Center of
the National Student Association, summaries of reform
programs sent out by the Student Press Association.

As a result, there is on most campuses an informed
body of educational opinion among the students, and
once the curriculum is opened up to the initiative of the

student body, the way is clear for a radical revision in the whole concept of student advising. That revision starts with the idea that what now happens informally in the exchange of ideas between students about their education and the life of the university should be made a central part of the teaching program. Undergraduates and graduate students who have shown talent and an informed interest can be appointed by the departments and the dean's office, and along with faculty members, can serve as advisers, with the student free to choose the person he would like to work with.

This revision in the advising system can also be linked to the various kinds of experimental colleges and free university programs in which students run their own affairs with the help of faculty members and other volunteers. On the basis of the information and ideas collected by students from each other as they discuss programs and possibilities for their own education, new ideas for the regular program—new courses, studies and ways of using the resources of the university—can be developed naturally and can be fed into the regular curriculum either through a Board for Educational Development as at Berkeley or through new undergraduate seminars as at the University of New Mexico.*

Once the course requirements have been removed, the matter of advising becomes crucial, especially for the freshmen. The advising for freshmen should actually begin while the student is still in high school and could become part of the way students are admitted to the university. That is, the undergraduate and graduate advisers could go to the high schools from which students are expected to come and through conferences, discussions and meetings held in regular class time, explore

* The undergraduate seminars and their role in possible reform at the University of New Mexico and elsewhere are discussed in Chapter 14.

the possibilities of what could be studied in the college
freshman year, and what kind of preparation in high
school is needed for various kinds of curricula. Each high
school student could be asked in his admission application
to outline a prospective program of studies which would
make sense to him and would build on what he was doing
in his junior and senior year in school. This would have
the reverse effect of making serious improvements in the
teaching and counselling system of the high school, and
any number of changes in course content and kinds of
studies would begin to occur as the teachers and students
began to consider what lay ahead in the first year of
college.

When the freshman comes to college he should begin
his college career with a freshman seminar designed to
explore the problems of learning in his new environment,
of how to make use of the resources of the university and
its surrounding community, and of how to relate to the
problems and issues of contemporary society and its educational and cultural system. In short, he should be given
a center in his freshman curriculum for exploration of
the concerns and needs of the beginning college student,
including the exploration of the curriculum most appropriate to his own goals, interests, and talents.

During the first days of his first week, the freshman
should spend most of his class time in this seminar, where
the question of what courses and teachers he should
choose would be the subject for group and individual discussion and conferences with his adviser. This would include not only the choice of courses but the variety of
alternatives one or another combination of courses could
offer in planning for a future career or in simply planning
for an education built around his strengths and interests.

This freshman seminar would be the student's center
of gravity in the whole first-year curriculum, the place
to which he could bring whatever problems he was concerned about, where he could make intellectual com-

panions and colleagues, and could count on a direct relation with one person responsible for him—the seminar leader—who could be a mature undergraduate, a selected graduate student, or a faculty member interested in students.

I cite the undergraduate and graduate seminar leaders, not only because in my experience, if the selection is made with care, talented students who put their minds to it can do this kind of teaching superbly well, but because the idea of freshman seminars is usually turned down by the departments and the dean's office who have no budget for small seminars for an entire freshman class, and there are too few faculty members who have an interest in or a talent for teaching them.

When the seminars are led by capable students, the students can be given course credit for the leaders and members alike, with the leaders given an appropriate stipend along with credit toward the graduate or undergraduate degree. The responsibility of these students for leading this kind of seminar is one of the best kinds of educational experiences they could have, aside from the contribution they make to the freshman students. It brings them into direct touch with the reality of student life and interests. It prepares them to become teachers of a new kind—the kind who see education as a coming-of-age and as the way in which students can teach themselves and one another with the help of teachers who understand how to teach this way.

9. Abolishing the Lecture System

Abolish the Lecture System as the Basic Method of Teaching and Substitute Other Kinds of Student Learning.

As in the case of the elimination of requirements, it is not so much the elimination of the lecture that is important, it is what is done in place of it once the way has been cleared for basic change. The lecture system is what is at fault, not the lecture, and I am not proposing the elimination of all lecture courses where those courses have a specific role to play in the whole range of educational methods.

The reasons for the change are obvious and stem from the simple fact that students learn very little on their own when they are being lectured to all the time. When the lecturer is brilliant and what he has to say is illuminating, when he makes new connections between ideas and demonstrates to his students the qualities of a first rate mind in action, he does something important in their education. This kind of scholar-teacher-talker is not the problem. The problem lies in making lecturing into a system in which the only kind of instruction the student ever gets is from someone talking from a podium.

Even if every teacher in every one of the five courses the student normally takes in a term were brilliant and the content of each of his lectures absorbing, three times a week in five separate courses means fifteen lectures a week. That is fifteen times a week that the student sits with his notebook, writing down what is said (or not said), and trying to remember from week to week what he *should* remember from his reading and the lectures.

On the face of it, that is an absurd way of teaching students to think and to learn for themselves. They learn *not* to think for themselves because the lectures do that for them. The lecturer interprets, summarizes, describes, lists points, defines, introduces general concepts, makes relationships. Sometimes, if he has talent approaching genius, he thinks aloud about a subject in which he is so thoroughly saturated that the lecture is an occasion on which new ideas are generated by the mere presence before him of a group of interested young people. That is the rare occasion. Most of the time the pedagogy is didactic, and merely covers "material" and sets things straight according to the canons of the academy.

When you think of the question, what *is* the student actually learning for himself, except in the rare instances when he is provoked into new thought by the inspiration of the lecturer? He is learning to record what the academic profession in a given field has decided to include in the consideration of its subject matter. That is also recorded in collateral textbooks, and, although it is hard to believe, most of the instruction through the lecture system is still tied directly to one textbook written by academic experts in the field, with a few other assignments in similar texts, not very many and with limited range. The limitation is necessary because the students themselves are limited in the time they can give to any one course or text, and the text and lectures have to be calibrated according to the average state of knowledge and capacity of the students in the course.

Under the lecture system it is also impossible to develop a community of persons within the course itself, no matter how many students sit together in the classroom. There is no occasion for the expression of commuity feeling or identity. You are in a class with fifty to one thousand or more other seated persons. When the class is over you leave and do not see any of the people you were with until the class meets again. Among the various needs common to all human beings is the need to be wanted, to be needed, and to become part of a community of persons with whom one feels at home. This is especially true of students in colleges and universities to which they come

at a time in their lives when they are not very sure of
themselves or of why they are there.

The passive role the students are condemned to occupy
in this kind of classroom prevents the development of
either personal or intellectual rapport. It is on the whole
a competitive situation in which the student tries to do
better in the tests than his fellows and uses his wits not
to learn but to survive in the competition. You cannot
feel a sense of identity with a community of scholars, as
the phrase goes, if you simply drive in to class three
times a week, park your car, or walk from the bus, go to
classes, and go home again or back to your paying job
as soon as the last class is over. There is no community
to feel an identity with. There is no opportunity to learn
from others if all you do is sit with them silently.

The art of teaching is the art of involving others in
one's own interests and taking an interest in theirs, and
the authority of the teacher rests on his qualities of mind
and character as these are seen in action. As in the case
of the psychiatrist and his patient, the result is measured
by how well the patient is able to carry on by himself
once the relationship is over. This means that in teaching,
the student must want to learn, just as the patient must
want to get well, and if this is not initially the case, the
first task for the teacher is to find ways in which the student can become involved in his own development and can
learn to want to cure himself from the mental disease of
ignorance.

To stand before students as a lecturer is of course one
way of having them come to know you, and it can be a
way of persuading those who have not yet learned to
learn. But the lecture system as it now works does not
involve the student in taking his own initiative. He is
taught to await instructions—how many pages to read
for next week, what papers to write, what to do in order
to succeed.

The question then is, what to do instead, while staying

within a teaching budget with fixed limits which show little sign of being extended in the future. Throughout the pages to follow there are proposals for ways of teaching and learning that replace the whole system of which lecturing is a part, and I will not repeat them here. They are proposals which start from the principle of involving students in their own learning, and they treat the lecture in that context as an instrument to be used sparingly in selected situations when it can serve that purpose.

One of the educational advantages of removing the lecture system is that it is then impossible to avoid thinking about live students and what to do with them. The educational problem shifts to two other matters—how to convey the information and ideas which at present the lecturer passes on through the spoken word, and how to design a schedule for a set of activities and experiences to give the most help to the student in learning what he needs to know.

The first of these, the communication of information, is not too difficult, and many answers have already been given, including the use of original materials in paperbacks rather than textbooks (although textbooks can sometimes be used for supplementary reading or as references), articles, tapes, films, records, and above all, the use of original written materials prepared by students and teachers through individual or joint research, then mimeographed, taped, spoken, danced, played, acted, painted, sculpted, and otherwise presented, both in the classroom and out of it.

The design of a learning schedule can also take a great many forms, depending on the field of study. In the case of dance or physics, or biology, there would be more emphasis on studio and laboratory work than, for example, in philosophy. Even here, however, since the laboratory of philosophy is in the community and the streets, there should be a good deal of field work in both those places.

But one basic pattern emerges from experiments with

non-lecture systems (again, taking for granted that the budget will not allow cutting down the size of classes so that they can be run informally). If the class is from 50 to 500 in size, it can meet once a week for one, or preferably two hours, and the rest of the week can be spent in student and faculty-led discussion groups and seminars, research in student teams, field work, reading, discussion in groups of two or three students on the reading, or in anything else that is planned by the teacher and the students.

The single meeting each week is the pivot around which the week turns and should be thought of as a kind of intellectual celebration to which everyone comes as a member of the class, where a program has been planned for the meeting from week to week. The faculty member would have the help of an elected or appointed steering committee of students to work out the agenda for the class meetings and to collaborate with him in the development of study topics, discussion groups, seminars, field work, and student teaching.

The weekly meeting might open with comments from the teacher on topics drawn from the student discussions, or the teacher might make a ten-minute presentation of a topic, with a question and answer period following, or it could be a student symposium where the panelists had been asked ahead of time to prepare short presentations of their own and to be ready to comment on the remarks of the teacher. The meeting time could also be used for a short film showing followed by a discussion or for visitors from elsewhere in the university or community, who would come to answer questions prepared in advance by the students on the basis of their reading of the visitor's work or their knowledge of his views as stated in mimeographed material distributed the previous week.

The weekly meeting would also leave time to deal with the educational details of the week's work, in a business session on what the members of the class expected to be doing that week, reports by discussion leaders, suggestions from the class as a whole. One of the conventional ways of organizing the rest of the week would be to assign each student to a student discussion group of ten to fifteen that met twice or perhaps three times; or, after the students learned to know each other in the first few discussions, they could be asked to choose two or three other students from the discussion groups to meet over dinner or in the evening to discuss the reading or the issues raised in the weekly meeting. The leadership of the discussion groups could be drawn from experienced undergraduate or graduate students, and during the semester, the faculty member in charge would visit the groups in sequence, as much as his time allowed, occasionally calling two or three of the groups together for joint sessions which he would lead.

10. Credit for What?

Revise Drastically the Present Academic Credit System,
and the Class Schedules to Which It Is Tied.

Were it not for the fact that academic crediting and its
units are now so thoroughly embedded in the record-
keeping and evaluation of university students that it is
impossible to eliminate it, except in the case of the experimental colleges, I would urge its complete abolition. But
I am trying to make practical suggestions for the reform
of the present system, and I believe it can be revised in
such a way that it will stop doing unnecessary harm to
student learning. One main way is to award over-all
credit for work in larger blocks of time and material.

To begin with, there is something inherently absurd in
the whole concept of academic credit, since it defines the
intellectual process as a series of fifty-minute units of
time spent in classrooms. Not only does this defy the
simple facts of psychology in its primitive definition of
what learning is and how the human mind works, but it
shores up all the other fallacies in the educational system,
from the lecture method to the interminable testing to
the numerical grading. The fact that we are dealing with
an administrative convenience rather than with a serious
educational principle is more glaringly obvious in the
case of academic crediting than it is in any other part of
the program of instruction. In the case of the lecture
system and course requirements, some sort of educational
defense can always be made. Academic crediting has nothing at all to recommend it except its convenience in keeping records.

Yet at the moment, it is the basic piece of machinery
that operates the system, since it not only defines what
education is but also controls what is allowed to happen
in its name. The three-credit course and the 120-credit
B.A. degree is the basis for nearly everything that is
done in the colleges, and so tight is the grip it holds over

the minds of faculty members and students alike that it
prevents creative thinking about other kinds of education which could be planned if educators were freed from
its bondage.

The issue has been raised in its most direct form
through the actions of students who have developed their
own student experimental colleges, community action
programs, tutorials, work-study projects, research plans,
and student courses, and who then ask that this kind of
education through student initiative be awarded credit
toward the degree. It has also come up through the experience of Peace Corps volunteers who, having taught
for two years in a foreign elementary school or high
school, ask for academic credit toward a teaching cer-
tificate, and are often told that it does not count because
the teaching was not carried out in an American school.
Or, as in the case of a faculty-approved course in the social sciences, initiated through regular channels by the
Berkeley students with Eldridge Cleaver as a lecturer, it
comes up when academic credit is disallowed on orders
from the Board of Regents.

The students are quick to point out that the units of
academic credit are not only tools to be used against the
reform of the system, but are, in a sense, a form of
money. Tuition is charged at so much a point of credit,
and the credit money is spent by the students for semester
hours of education in about the same way one would go
about buying a refrigerator or reserving a hotel room.

On the other hand, once academic crediting is seen for
what it is, and the question has been raised about what
counts for credit and what does not, the way is clear for
serious discussion of what should be included in a college
education. Granted the fact that merely to stay alive is
highly educational, a distinction has to be made at some
point between what people ordinarily do from day to day
and what they should do if they are members of a college

student body. There are many things that are beneficial
to personal development—marriage, raising children,
running a rock band—but not necessarily as part of the
college curriculum.

One of the things young people are finding out for
themselves is that there *are* some very important educational experiences to be had outside the educational institutions. A good many students are staying out of college
for a year or two, working at a job, living in a commune,
travelling and studying on their own, going to concerts,
the theater, art galleries, museums, tutoring children,
working in VISTA, and are finding that a rangier attitude
to their own education is a first step toward improving
its quality. To break out of the pattern of sixteen years
of class-going is, in itself, a step ahead.

The experimental colleges—Antioch, Bennington, Sarah
Lawrence, Friends World College, Goddard, among others
—assume that the world is the campus and that the
college is a central learning space with which the student
is identified and where he can make his intellectual and
educational home. He moves out from that center with its
libraries, laboratories, teachers, and courses into the surrounding cultures, institutions and communities in order
to learn by direct experience what is going on there, and
brings back what he has learned to add to what he can
continue learning on the college campus. In these experimental colleges, the question of academic credit for what
the students do is settled by whether or not the experience, on and off the campus, is of a kind which advances
the student's intellectual, aesthetic, and cultural growth.
A special effort is made in planning periods of time in
field work, non-resident terms, community action programs, and individual student projects to increase the
range of the student's experience beyond the academic
limits of the conventional system.

When education is redefined in this way as a body of
experience and not simply as a body of academic knowl-

edge, the academic credit system falls into its proper place as a convenient way of keeping track of what the student does. At Sarah Lawrence College, for example, where there are no grades, examinations, or units of academic credit, an experimental program was begun in the 1950's in the education of elementary school teachers. According to state requirements, various amounts of academic credit were to be assigned for work in the philosophy and history of education, psychology, practice teaching, etc. Since a regular program at Sarah Lawrence involves work in three areas or courses in a given year, and since a four-year, 120-credit B.A. degree would therefore involve thirty credits a year, the college simply assigned ten units of credit for a year's work in the area of the requirement and went ahead unchanged with the combination of field work, classroom study, student projects, and direct teaching experience which made up the content of the experimental program. There was no need to alter the program simply because credits were to be given for it.

That sort of approach works very well in the revision of the standard college schedule of three-credit classes, once educators rid themselves of the notion that everything has to be cut in the same size from the same academic cloth. All that is required is that the general budgeting of the student's time be arranged so that he is not running from class to class in five different courses a semester. The system as it now works cuts against the possibility that teachers and students can ever spend enough consecutive time working together at one subject or topic to go deeply into the matters they are studying. It also prevents teachers and students from doing anything other than meeting in the classroom, since there is literally no time for field trips, group research, informal conferences, discussions, or community projects—it is all taken up in the classroom meetings and the reading assignments that go with them.

In fact, one of the most frequent complaints made by students, especially those who are most serious, is that they can never do justice to any single subject because their time is spread over so many different ones. A revision of the course offerings and styles of teaching, to allow time for a mixture of methods and experience, could arrange for three and four courses as the normal number to be taken at once, with five credits to be given for each, without specifying how many of the hours in the work of the course must be spent in class meetings. This could be decided by the teacher and his students as they plan their work together. Even under the present system, this is often done under the heading of double-credit courses and similar devices. All that is necessary is to extend the idea and make a general practice out of what is now the exception.

There is also a great deal to be done in revising the whole pattern of scheduling in the semester system in which, as of now, everyone assumes that each week of each term has to be identical in style and experience with every other—the three-credit-three-classroom-meetings syndrome once again. If over-all credit is granted for a full term of work in a given field, with the amount of credit to be decided by the amount of work a student is asked to do and the time it takes to do it, a whole series of innovations can be set in motion. A faculty member in sociology could take a class of thirty students into a community away from the campus for a non-resident term of direct study of the institutions of that community. A biologist could do a comparable project in ecology with his students, as could an anthropologist, an economist, a social psychologist. It would be up to the faculty member to satisfy himself that what his students learned met the standards of the intellectual community of which he is a part, and to award credit accordingly.

On the campus itself, there is no reason why direct

study in the field cannot be combined with work in classes, discussion groups, student research and student-led seminars, especially in subjects that have to do with education, the schools, practice teaching, tutorials, and social change. In the case of freshmen, why not take the time to have them study themselves and their education, through the freshmen seminars, using the university environment and their own place in it as the source for the materials of internal field work?

Or in an even simpler form, the single course on the campus without field work can be scheduled so that the first two or three weeks concentrate on two or three major topics studied intensively, the next three weeks move into more general areas, with the last six to eight weeks given to individual student projects which the students have been asked to work out as they have become more familiar with the field of study through the things they did in the earlier part of the semester. As I have already pointed out, there could be one meeting of the full class each week to serve as a central pivot around which the course would turn, with student reports to the class, talks by the teacher and by selected visitors, question and answer sessions, or whatever seemed to the teacher and a volunteer steering committee of students to be the best use of the time when everyone came together. The rest of the course time could be spent in discussion groups, group research, working through an annotated bibliography, and individual study projects.

Many other things can be done to change the static quality of the present five-course system and to bring a different rhythm into the college year. When the semester patterns have been changed in the past, they have usually been shifted from a two-semester fifteen-week period with summer sessions, to either a three-semester or a quarter year, quite often with the quarter year courses trying to do in ten weeks what was formerly done in fifteen. Again, the problem of dividing up the year has

been looked at from the point of view of administrative
convenience, not educational principle.

This is not the case among the educators who have
argued for, and sometimes installed, a year in which
there are two full terms, one in the fall from September
to December, the other in the winter and spring, from
mid-February to mid-June, with a four-week intercession
in January and February. Here the plan, based on the
natural rhythm of time, pauses at Christmas, and elimi-
nates the lame duck period of January which is a kind of
leftover of the fall term, and makes no educational sense,
since it is usually spent in winding up the previous term's
courses and administering examinations.

The intelligent use of an intercession of four weeks
gives the students a chance either to do non-resident work
of a specified kind, usually student initiated, or to use
the campus as a place for intensive work in political,
social, educational or cultural issues, with a complete
break from the conventional course patterns of the rest
of the year. Sometimes an arts festival is included, with
the first three weeks spent by students and faculty preparing exhibits, plays, choreography, film shows, discussion programs, culminating in a week's festival or conference. At other times, departments or divisions of the
college take on special projects which they work out with
their students. It is a great time for the kind of educational experiment which should really be going on all
year. It calls upon the resourcefulness of the faculty and
students to do something interesting and educationally
useful that they can't do under the regular program.
Academic credit is awarded simply by counting whatever
the college does in this period as part of the students'
education.

The idea of the intercession can be expanded into a
point of view about the use of time in the regular se-
mesters, as can the idea of summer sessions that break

with the usual educational methods and take on four- to six-week periods of special work in chosen fields, especially in the arts. In the case of those colleges which made plans in the May strike period of 1970, the twenty colleges which decided on a two-week interval to allow time for political action by students and faculty in the November elections broke with the standard pattern of thinking about what makes a college education and what is worthy of the award of academic credit.

The extension of this kind of educational thinking could create a new range of alternatives to the regular course sequences and the obligatory use of standard credit hours. It could include, for example, the week-long arts festival, or weekend festivals and conferences directly related to the work going on during the courses, or a week or two to three days in which the regular courses are suspended and the entire community can spend time together going over the problems of educational reform and the issues of student life. These issues erupt at other times during the college year, but no time is allowed for considering them, on the assumption that so serious an interest in social, political, or educational issues is abnormal and should not deflect the student from the proper business of his daily education.

But above all, it seems to me that the revision of the credit-giving attitude can have its most lasting and important effect in taking seriously the initiative of students in building their own courses and starting their own educational programs. I watched with interest and delight the development of the student experimental college at San Francisco State, beginning in 1965, and found in it a model for the imaginative reform of college education. The student college began in the interests of the students and their work in the community on everything from tutoring children in the slums to putting together new programs in Black Studies and the arts. It served as a

way of introducing new courses and ideas into the regular
San Francisco State curriculum, since a vote of the faculty made it possible to award credit toward the degree
for any student courses or programs which a faculty
member agreed to supervise.

This meant, as it has meant elsewhere when the student reform movement has been taken seriously, that
there was a continuous flow of educational thinking in
the student body, as well as a practical arrangement
through which that thinking could inject itself into the
stream of educational change. In this situation, students
are encouraged to become involved, their ideas are valued,
their relation to the faculty becomes one in which they
and their teachers are colleagues working together. Although there will be dispute, debate, and controversy
about what kind of student work should be legitima-
tized by academic credit, the supreme advantage is that it
keeps the debate about education alive in the normal
course of events, and not confined to crisis periods when
outbreaks of student protest against college educational
policy raise the issues with which the college should be
concerned all along.

LEWIS AND CLARK COLLEGE LIBRARY
PORTLAND,   OREGON   97219

11. Testing, Grading, and Failing

Eliminate the Present Grading and Testing System and Work Out New Ways of Judging Student Accomplishments

It is hard to know where to begin in saying what is wrong with the grading system since its effects are so pervasive and its connections with the rest of the system so complete that no matter where you start you come back to the same point—that there is no worthy educational principle in it. Once more we are face to face with an administrative device and another absurdity, this time a combination of abacus and computer to measure intellectual success and failure in numerical units. Yet its power as an educational killer is enormous.

In order to be understood correctly, the present university teaching program should not be looked at as education at all but as a communication system. What is to be communicated is decided by the course requirements and academic credits, how it should be communicated is decided by the lecture system, the extent to which the communication has been received and recorded is measured by the testing and grading apparatus. Because it controls decisions about the worth of student accomplishment, the assignment of grades controls everything else, and is responsible, more than anything else, for injecting the twin poisons of hypocrisy and fear of failure into the student consciousness.

When students speak of being imprisoned in the present system, there is reality in the metaphor. They are often told by their teachers that grades do not matter, that it is learning that counts. But they quickly learn that learning does not count and grades do, since learning, no matter what the teachers say, is measured by grades, and the student with low grades is considered to be a failure. He learns to think of himself that way.

Although it is possible to argue that any intelligent and competent student can beat the system and need not worry about his tests and scores, that is not the point, even if and when it is true. An average or below-average student is as important an educational responsibility for the educator as the above-average, and when one calculates that at least ninety-five percent of all students have to be average and below average before there can be a minority which is above average, the responsibility rests with the educator to teach in such a way that all his students are encouraged to learn, not merely those who compete for the honors.

In any case, so much has been written about the evils of grading and testing, and the connection they have with the defects of education that it is not necessary to rehearse the entire subject again. There is a growing body of such literature written by students, and increasing protest against the system by the student reformers and activists on the campuses. There is also a growing body of research which describes the effects of grading on the educational system at large, from elementary school on. Most of it shows the negative results of grading practices and the lack of meaning in the numerical grade itself, especially when these are joined to the points of academic credit and the ridiculous figure called the grade point average is worked out to two and three decimal points.

One of the best short summaries of the problem of the grading system as seen by students was written by Miss Susan Wyatt in the spring of 1970 for the Educational Reform Center, the student-run reform program of the National Student Association. Miss Wyatt's essay refers to a cross-section of research on the subject, including

Donald P. Hoyt's work in demonstrating the lack of relationship between grades in college and personal, professional, or business success in later life. After describing her case for abolishing the grading system, Miss Wyatt quotes from a research project which sums up most student judgment as I know it about the bad effects of the system. The research was carried out by Ronald Burke with students at the University of Minnesota and showed that 7.9 percent of the students thought grades helped learning, 65.8 percent thought grades interfered with learning, and 26.3 percent were undecided. The students who thought the grades interfered gave a range of reasons which included:

1. The extreme importance attached to good grades results in grades, not knowledge or learning, becoming the prime interest of the student.

2. Grades are not the real value of the course; its real value lies in use and application of what is learned later on in life.

3. Emphasis on grades makes one take courses in which he can get good grades instead of courses he is interested in.

4. Grades handicap the teacher, requiring him to teach things he can measure. The teacher is no longer seen as a "helper" but as a critic.

5. Grades create the frustration of receiving bad grades. The pressure and anxiety over grades makes learning unpleasant and impossible.

6. The student learns only what he feels will be on the test and does his best to outguess the teacher.

7. The student is afraid to make mistakes, appear stupid or displease the instructor.

8. Grades drive the student to dishonesty.

9. Grades force class attendance and encourage memorizing and cramming for the test followed by eventual forgetting.

I would agree that most of these comments are accurate, and I would say that student opinion in general coincides with the opinions of Burke's Minnesota sample. It also coincides with the opinion of quite a few faculty members and a large number of deans, many of whom are tired of hearing the flow of familar comment on the subject, since they have been hearing it and recognizing it for a good many years.

In some cases, rebel faculty members have simply refused to assign grades, and in more than one instance have been dismissed for their rebellion, or have raised such a controversy with such unilateral action that they have been ignored by their colleagues and accused of simply trying to get attention and publicity. In discussions on the campuses, my reply to that has been that no matter how the issue was raised or by whom, the more publicity on the subject the better, since wherever I went I found faculty members and students who agreed with one another and with me about how bad the system was, but who seldom acted to change it.

Sometimes I met critics of the grade system who had stopped fighting it after having taught experimental courses in which they announced at the beginning of the course that class attendance was not required and that no grades would be awarded. They then found that half the class dropped out at the beginning because the students did not want to run the risk of not having a grade on their transcripts and preferred the regular system of class meetings, lectures, and everything as before. They also found that only a handful of students came to class, and the most intelligent and honest of those who stayed away pointed out that with all the other pressures on them from the other courses where they had to fight for grades, they could not afford the time and energy, much as they would have liked to, to work very much in a course taught without compulsory attendance or grades.

They said frankly that they needed the time to give to the courses where it counted. Having tried and been chagrined by the results of the trial, teachers who liked the idea of reforming the system returned to the regular methods and tried to do the best they could with them.

Other faculty members told me that they had no interest in ever trying or allowing such foolishness. Certainly the system was bad, and certainly it had all the defects I said it had. But the students had been so conditioned by the mythology of grading, testing and academic competition in high school and college that to try to decondition them by abolishing the grading system or revising the whole examination, credit and lecture arrangement was impossible.

The students, they said, would not work if there were no grades, and for the students' own good the grading had to be kept in the system. When I asked for the empirical evidence that supported that statement and wanted to know how much they knew about the motivation of their present students, aside from future students who might be taught without being graded, the answer was that the students' motivation was simply to take the course to get credit and a grade toward the degree. If they learned something as well, that was all to the good. The number of students involved was too large in the state colleges and universities to do anything but mass-produce them, and while teaching without examinations, required courses, grades, or lectures might be possible at expensive small colleges like Sarah Lawrence and Bennington, that system could never be applied to mass education.

This is simply not true. If the non-grading system were applied to mass education it would work very well there, not in the same form that it takes in smaller colleges, but according to the same principles. It is truer to say that the present attitude to education held by the faculty makes it impossible to persuade them as the policy-makers of the present system to shift to something different. The shift involves a complete reversal of the idea of the curriculum as a communication system to the idea of the curriculum as something created by students as they work with their teachers. Not many faculty members are ready for that, even though they may be sympathetic to modest reforms.

But the situation is very serious. Even the opponents of change will agree that the true spirit of learning can only be reached by those who are so absorbed in what they are doing that the learning becomes important in itself—for the sheer intellectual reward of discovering what one can discover, from knowing what there is to be known. It seems to me the grossest form of irresponsibility and cheap cynicism to know this to be true, and yet at the same time refuse to change a system generally acknowledged as one which makes it all but impossible either to experience the delight of knowing and discovering for its own sake or to learn how to gain this kind of experience.

The students are put into competition with one another. Instead of cooperating and helping each other to learn, they are deliberately taught by the system to negate the true values of the intellect and of serious and committed intellectual enterprise. If that is not a serious enough reason for changing the system, we have exhausted the possibility of even talking about the improvement of education.

Suppose the faculty, recognizing the need for radical reform of the testing and grading system, decided that from this point on no grades would be given. Students who met the standards of the course would pass. But those who, for whatever reason, could not meet the standards appropriate to the work would not fail. They simply would not have the fact they they had taken the course recorded on their transcript. Ostensibly their purpose in taking the course in the first place was to learn what there was to be learned in it, and if they have not managed to do that, they should be neither penalized nor rewarded.

Would this change in the grading and testing system mean that students would immediately lose interest in working? Not if the work were interesting and they were being taught not only how to learn what they needed to know but how to judge how well they were learning it. To those who argue that only through competition of the kind that is engrained in their consciousness through years of bad education in the schools can the students be expected to try hard, the reply is that if they are that competitive and can work only under the competition of the grade, they are suffering from a sinister educational disease from which they need to be cured if they are ever to be able to enjoy the work of the mind and to look at themselves as persons with ideas of their own.

Or to put it another way, if they are so steeped in the spirit of competition, will they lose their wish to excel simply because there is no numerical symbol to point to as a sign of their achievement? They don't look for numbers in the other parts of their lives. They appreciate the approval of their friends, fellow students and others in dozens of ways and places where there are no numbers attached.

In my experience, students in free non-competitive educational environments simply develop other and more intense motivations. They find no need to compete, except with themselves. They want to do increasingly better work and they are helped by the comparisons they learn to make with the work of others. They are ready to go to others, including their teachers, for help. Once the educational air has been cleared and the teacher no longer has either the responsibility or power to classify them into derogatory categories (anything lower than an A means you are not all you should be), a completely new set of motivations develops, and the whole atmosphere changes, especially if the lecture system is either thrown out or greatly modified. Those who do not do any work and fail the course, or do work hard and still fail, are in the same position in a gradeless course as they would be in a graded one, except that if there were informal discussion groups and some of the other tutorial arrangements of a student-centered course, all of them would get more help in learning what was offered to them to know.

As for the technical problem of deciding, without grades, who is qualified for graduate work or for admission to a given undergraduate department, there are many better ways of deciding that than by counting up grade point averages. This seems to me to be the worst way. One alternative would obviously be the recommendation of teachers who could not avoid noticing talented students. Another, in the new system, would be the nomination or recommendation by other students. Another would be a fairly open-ended questionnaire, interviews, or a statement by the student of what he wants to study, why, and how he would go about it if admitted.

Employers who want to know about class standing, grades, and the rest, would be much better off if compelled, in the absence of such information, to work out their own ways of selecting their employees. Much of the time they lose good candidates for jobs, especially among the minority groups, because the absence of a high-scoring academic record prevents candidates who are otherwise qualified from applying.

On the whole, I found more deans and administrators than faculty members interested in radical or at least progressive reforms in the grading and testing system. Many of the administrators said that if the faculty would start some serious experiments or at least some serious thinking about the changes that could be made, as far as they were concerned they not only had no objection but would welcome the chance to include the changes in the university structure. Where the proposals usually broke down was in the simple practical question of what to do instead.

At smaller colleges it is quite true that when the relations between the faculty and students are fairly close and the teachers have a chance to know directly what their students are doing through their work together, written reports to the students can be substituted for grades, and no testing or examining is necessary, since both the student and teachers have a good idea of the progress made by each.

In the large university it seems unlikely that that kind of close relation with teachers will ever be possible. In fact, it seems more likely as of now, with budgets either cut or not expanded to deal with the expansion in student numbers, that there will be even less chance of having enough faculty members to go around. Whatever solutions are to be found for revision of grading and testing are going to have to take this fact into account.

The most radical change in the system as a whole would therefore be to revise completely the role of the student in his own education, and to look at learning not as the communication of a body of knowledge but as what the student does with his time and energy. If the student is never given the freedom and responsibility to learn things for himself, he is unlikely to do much more than take what he is given without comment and without using it for his own intellectual growth. Nor is he likely to learn how to reach an informed opinion about his own ability as a student, or even about his identity as a person if that judgment is continually made by others in the mechanical way that now prevails. Until he can recognize within himself the quality of his own achievement, he is at the mercy of his social and academic environment, and of a system which operates at present in such a way that all the emphasis is on external judgment for the use of record-keeping, not on the internal judgments and psychic growth of the learner. Learning and judging the quality of the learning are two parts of the same enterprise.

The question of testing and grading should be reduced to the question of how the student can learn to judge his own ability, and whatever changes are made in the system must start with that as their aim. Luckily, it is true that students learn a great deal from each other. Part of this is a matter of the atmosphere in which they live as students. If the intellectual environment is invigorating, friendly, cooperative, and sympathetic rather than, as it is now, competitive, dehumanized, over-organized, and, in a deep sense, anti-intellectual, the influence students have on each other in what and how they learn is immeasurably increased.

It is for this reason that I propose a program of student teaching, not in the formal sense of replacing the faculty by students, but by simply taking for granted the fact that no matter what else is true, students are already a greater actual and potential influence on each others' attitudes, ideas, motivations, and interests than are the members of a distant faculty. The students now form a body of independent social opinion and educational action. They have already been teaching each other about education, through their own research studies, reports, critiques, student conferences, and educational programs. They do not need to give each other tests and assign grades to know who should have an A in educational reform or anything else. They judge each other by performance.

One simple way to take advantage of student-teaching talent would be to extend to its full the cooperation of the faculty with the student experimental college movement, and to take the idea which lies behind it, of student-initiated courses, projects and programs, as a basic instrument of educational change and instruction. This would not only help to remake the present curriculum, but by involving students in the teaching, it would make a new kind of relationship between the faculty and the students. As of now the curriculum and the courses are made by the academic departments and the faculty curriculum committees, with the sanction of the dean's office. In some cases students are consulted, or are members of faculty curriculum committees. The next step, without waiting for the students to start their own experimental colleges, would be to call on the students to help organize their own courses in collaboration with their teachers, and to organize their own groups for learning inside the courses, choosing, with the help of the teacher, the students who would act as discussion leaders and teaching assistants.

The faculty member would be responsible to the university administrative officers for the quality and content of the course, but it would be up to him to decide, in the last analysis, whether the work going on met the standards of university education. In the experience of those who have worked this way, the students have quite often reverted to conventional styles of teaching and learning, even to the point of wanting to retain some version of the grading system. In other cases, where the assignment of a grade is mandated by the administration, and sometimes demanded by the regional accrediting agencies, ways have been found of testing and grading which eliminate the negative effects of the grading system itself.

In other cases, the situation on a given campus is such that there is little chance that radical change in the teaching system is possible—there are not enough concerned and reform-minded teachers and administrators to start up the game. But even here there are quite a few non-radical and feasible changes in the grading system which can be introduced.

That is to say, if a grade must be assigned, it can be

a letter grade based on a whole variety of criteria, including the initiative shown by the student, the amount of time and energy he has put into his work, the quality of his leadership inside his own group, the quality of his writing, or of his research, the quality of his questions as well as of his answers and the extent of his contribution to the course itself. If the administration were willing, an arrangement could be made by which students in any course could choose whether or not they wished to take the course on a pass-fail basis or to be graded by whatever methods they and their teacher worked out together. These could include a final examination, written or oral, or the presentation of a body of work completed over the term, or a presentation to the class or to one part of it. It could be an examination in which the student chose the topics he wished to be examined on.

The virtue in this approach to the grading problem is that it faces the student with the necessity of deciding how he wishes to be judged and includes him in the process of the judging. The "average" or "poor" student would turn out to be a student who, for whatever reason —lack of motivation, lack of previous experience and training, unfamiliarity with anything but the conventional courses, or lack of academic ability—did not respond to the situation and did not accomplish very much.

But at the very least, he would have had his chance, he could call upon the help of his classmates, he would not be penalized by the system if he asked ignorant questions, he would not be under the constant fear of the grade he might receive since in large part it would be self-administered and would depend on the degree of his own involvement in what he had agreed to do.

Even without the revision of the teaching system to include students fully in the course planning and teaching, a great deal can be done by individual faculty members or groups of faculty members working together to revise the way their classes are conducted. Suppose in a course in the social sciences or the humanities in which there were a hundred students, the class meetings, as in the example I have used before, were reduced to one a week, the rest of the time to be used in student discussion groups and individual work with the help of undergraduate and graduate students selected and appointed by the teacher. Students could be asked to write short papers on selected topics for the use of their own discussion groups, with the papers mimeographed or dittoed so that each member of the group could have a copy.

Since this sort of paper is written to be used by other students rather than to be presented to the faculty member for grading, it creates a completely different attitude on the part of the student who writes it. It is not that he will become less responsible for the quality of what he says in his paper because it is not written to be graded. He will in most cases become *more* responsible, since he is presenting himself to fellow students who will let him know very quickly what they think of what he says. By the end of the term, each student will have put together a body of his own work, some of it rewritten after he has heard it discussed in his group, and he will have a fairly accurate idea of how good it is.

Another way of combining the learning with the judging is to ask each student to keep work sheets on what he has done during the term, with descriptions of and comments on the books he has read, the research he has done, the time he has spent. These would be mimeographed and shared with the other members of his group and the teacher. Very soon comparisons begin to be made between the work of one student and another. Ideas are exchanged for improving the use of the students' time, and the comments in the work sheets on the books read or research done generate other comments by students whose reading and experience produced different conclusions. The teacher, on his part, learns a great deal more about his students and what they are learning from looking over the work sheets and the papers written for other students than he would from reading examination papers from or the results of objective tests.

An extension of the work sheet idea can also be made by asking the students to keep a daily journal of comments on what is being learned, notes on books, on the discussion sessions, on the comments of other students, on what the teacher has said, or on anything else he is thinking or doing that he believes is worth recording. Students can also be asked to bring in questions, articles, ideas, comments from others to his group for their use either as topics for discussion or as pieces of general information. In combination with any other criteria the faculty member wishes to introduce, the work sheets and journals can be used as the basis for assigning a letter grade at the end of the term. Or, better still, this way of teaching and judging might be tried as an experiment in which no grade was assigned at all, and students wrote brief reports about their judgment of the work of other students in the group.

Other colleges have experimented with awarding the grade of passing or failing in selected courses, usually only one out of the four or five courses taken in a term. This has fairly limited usefulness as an experiment in freer or gradeless learning, since it is likely to suffer from the same problem as the single course in which the gradeless teacher finds his students working harder and better for someone else no matter how much they enjoy the work with him.

When undergraduates present their transcripts for admission to graduate school, or for whatever other purpose they present them, the single courses with no grade to recommend them constitute a handicap, or if they don't, the students are afraid they will. In order to reap its results, the idea of pass-fail grading should be carried more broadly into the whole system, along with some of the other reforms that naturally go with it. In the meantime, the failure of the pass-fail arrangement in single instances should not be counted as evidence against its merit.

On the whole, it seems to me that the best strategy for change as far as grading is concerned is simply to start doing things which help to neutralize the bad effects of the grading practices. If student reformers and faculty members content themselves with denouncing grades, and then find that there is little chance of persuading anyone to abolish them, there is nowhere to go except into frustration. I think that student and faculty reformers will get farther with this issue if they concentrate on immediate modification of testing and grading and shifts in the style of teaching toward student-centered learning in collaboration with those faculty members who are already interested in moving in that direction.

Many of the faculty members whose reluctance to change makes such moves impossible have never thought seriously of what they might do instead of what they are now doing. They like the present system because it works, they are used to it, and in most cases have never known or thought about any other. Theirs is usually not a willful opposition, but one based on their own experience, and they honestly fear that if their control of the course and of student work in it were given up by the abolition of grades and testing, the course would go to pieces and there would be no solid accomplishment by their students.

One immediate and conservative modification could be to increase the number of small group meetings each week, decrease the number of lectures or meetings of the full class and eliminate the concept of the "quiz" section and the mid-semester examination. Since the objective test measures only the retrieval capacity of students, it should be eliminated, or used, not as part of the grading system, but as an educational instrument in the hands of the student and teacher to find out whether the student has the information in his head that he needs for his education. In fact, if all testing and examining were reduced to a minimum and thought of as ways in which students can be made aware of what they know, much of the negative effect of testing could be eliminated. It is because the testing is directly linked to grading and is not conceived as an aid to the student in his learning that the evil sets in.

I have seen courses organized with students making up their own tests, reading and criticizing each other's papers, carrying out joint research projects in teams, and deciding for themselves how they wanted to be judged, with the teacher in the position of helping them to judge, while retaining the ultimate authority of decision as to the measure of their accomplishment. At the very least in such a reorganization of the teaching pattern, the students are relieved of the neurosis which makes them continually ask before paying attention to whatever is said or done, Will this be on the test? The educational malpractice of teaching to the test will continue to corrupt the system as long as testing is treated as a means of grading students rather than as a means of helping them to discover what they know and can do.

Support for this view has now come from a source close to the center of the entire testing movement—the College Entrance Examination Board—whose testing devices have been heavily criticized over the years by the progressive wing of the educational reform movement. A twenty-one-member Commission on Tests, after a three year study of the educational effects of the testing system, issued a report in November of 1970, pointing out that the college board examinations as well as other kinds of tests and examinations constantly in use have a stultifying influence on the education of students.

The commission recommends drastic reforms in the present testing programs, including a new approach to the idea of testing, with the emphasis placed on helping the student to discover his own potential and on introducing a whole new series of criteria for educational aptitudes—talent in the arts, for example, capacity for intellectual and social leadership, motivation for learning, ability to adapt to new situations.

In short, the commission recommends that educational accomplishment be measured throughout the full range of the student's intellectual and personal ability, and that success in high school and college must no longer be measured by criteria which operate in the narrow dimension of the formal academic skills. The applications of the Commission's recommendations on a broad scale throughout the high schools and colleges can have a profound effect on the reform of the curriculum and teaching methods presently in use.

Any imaginative revision of tests and examinations will turn up alternatives, and will turn the idea of testing as a form of anxious hovering over the student into the idea of the student testing himself against the reality of his own ability. If a student were asked in a psychology course to learn to know a six-year-old child and to write an account of what games he plays, what other children he knows, what television programs he sees, and what he gets from them, this would be a form of test, and one from which the student would learn a good deal. Or if he were asked to teach a child who was having trouble with reading and to make a report on what seemed to be the root of the problem and how he set about trying to help solve it, that would be a test. The report need not be counted as a part of the grading system. It would be simply a part of the student's education, and the content of what the student learned would be the test of whether or not it had been a good assignment in the first place.

If faculty members and educational institutions continue to insist on final examinations as a means of deciding whether or not a student is qualified, and that seems at the moment to be most likely, there is a full variety of change possible in the nature of final examinations. They do not have to be one, two or three-hour written examinations in which the intent is to catch the student in not knowing things which have been covered in the course. They could be for some students a one-or-two-day writing project in which they were asked to prepare a report on a given topic relevant to the nature of the course, using whatever books, outlines, help from other students, or anything else which seemed useful, as part of the project.

For others, an arrangement might be made for a research project carried on during the latter half of the course, culminating in a written report on a final date; or a conventional written examination whose questions had been worked out ahead of time by the students and their teacher together; or in the natural sciences, it might consist in a written description by the student of how he would organize and perform a given experiment in physics, chemistry, or biology, with a series of topics for such experiments prepared by the teacher ahead of time.

There are other ways. Suppose in the social sciences, the arts and the humanities, the use of taped interviews, and the use of tapes and original recordings of all kinds were a regular part of the system of learning and teaching. It would be sensible to allow the production of a taped documentary on film or on recorder to be presented as a form of final examination, just as it has seemed sensible to others in the field of literature and writing to accept novels, short stories, plays, and poems, along with critical essays, as the equivalent of examinations. This is equally true in the visual arts, where a mixture of written work and works in sculpture, design, painting, and electronic mixed-media experiments are welcome as examples of the student's accomplishment.

In other words, the examining of students to decide on their virtues and defects should be part of their education, not the arbiter of their future. The kind of examining must therefore vary according to the nature of the learning. It would be absurd to judge the dance student or the theater student by the same criteria one would judge a physics or engineering student, although the philosophy of examining remains constant. The test of worth is to be seen in the performance of the student *as* a physicist, an engineer, a dancer, a writer, or an actor, and these are all different kinds of performances to be seen and judged in different ways.

In the case of the performing arts, the situation is more obvious than in some other fields. When dancing and choreography are the field of study, it is clear that students, to be counted as having learned what they set out to learn, should be able to dance, to compose dances, and to know something about the use of the body as an aesthetic instrument and to be able to demonstrate what they have learned to their teachers. That is not a question to be answered on a written examination. What they are able to do at the end of a term or a year of study will not come as a surprise to their teachers. The progress or lack of it will have been obvious throughout the whole period of learning, and a great deal depends on what the student brings to the art form in the first place. What might be extraordinary progress in one student who started without much talent or skill would be less than satisfactory in a student who started at a higher level. This is also true of students in other fields, although very little account is taken of that fact.

Above all, it is the improvement of the education of the student that is at stake, not the improvement in the sophistication of the testing and grading program. The more that that is kept in mind, the closer we are likely to come to the day when testing and grading will actually be abolished as bad education and a waste of time.

12. Education Through Art

Give Every Student a Full Opportunity to Work in One or More of the Creative Arts as a Normal Part of the Undergraduate Curriculum.

Once the subject matter requirements for the B.A. degree are removed, the way is open to deal directly with one of the most important problems in the undergraduate curriculum—the absence of experience in the arts for most of the students who graduate. Plays are talked about in drama courses in the English department, painting and sculpture in art history courses, in humanities courses, but except in the physical education department where students can dance if they must and in some speech departments where there are theater classes, there is no expectation either by the student or the university that his education will include the practice of the arts themselves. Those with special interests in music, theater, design, architecture, painting, sculpture, or dance enroll in the professional programs or the college of fine arts, the rest go along to their classes, read the assignments, write their examinations, and graduate with entire areas of experience essential to their intellectual and personal growth left untouched.

It is one of the ironies of the present system of requirements that it makes certain that each student has studied the subject matter of the natural sciences, the social sciences and the humanities on the assumption that without knowledge in these major fields one cannot be considered well educated, while ignoring completely the need of the human being for experience in creating something of his own. In making these requirements the universities have said something about what they think a human life should be. They are saying that it is not possible to live life to the full or take a useful place in society unless you have read a set of assigned

120

books, listened to the lectures and proven that you can
remember what was written and what was said.

This does a very great disservice to the student. Not
only does it hoodwink the student into thinking that
that is what education amounts to. It teaches him that
that is what life is—a series of dutiful gestures toward
unexamined obligations. It neglects the education of his
senses and his feelings, and gives him the idea that the
arts are something done by artists, just as science is
something done by scientists, and that no one except
the exceptional should meddle in them as part of his
education.

When the requirements have been removed, the same
general assumptions are likely to be made. Students will
go on assuming that the arts are frills and real education
is in the sciences and humanities taught to them in
courses. It is time to say, and to act upon the saying,
that the creative arts are basic to all education, and
that they should be in the curriculum provided for all
students from elementary school through the undergraduate years. The creative arts are basic because they
provide a way in which each person can become himself,
and can extend himself in imagination to something other
than he is. Even a glance at what is now done in the
colleges will show that this is not the intention of the
program, not simply because the arts are left out, but
because the total effect of doing what you are asked to
do by the curriculum is to dampen the creative urge no
matter where it tries to assert itself, in the social and
natural sciences or anywhere else.

This is one of the reasons the students have been
looking for their own alternatives to the present curriculum. They apply the idea of relevance across a broad
sweep of intellectual and aesthetic actions. When they
look for ways of discovering themselves in encounter

groups or in sensitivity training, for example, they are making up for lacks in their own education. They are defining relevance as forms of experience which mean something to them personally. A subject of study or a form of educational experience becomes relevant when it speaks to their own concerns, and one of their concerns as students is with the development of themselves both in relation to others and to the exploration of consciousness. Much of what they do and wish to do about such exploration is amateurish, which is all in its favor, since it therefore remains honest and is willing to grope toward its own kind of self-discovery and its own kind of psychic truth.

Many of the students have come to an interest in the arts through growing up in the youth culture, and when they find that the works of art in the college humanities courses are treated as famous objects about which they are required to have information, they simply cannot gain aesthetic or intellectual nourishment from what they are asked to do. Their interest in the arts is not an interest in becoming scholars, art historians, museum curators, or gallery directors, although some may learn to become interested in those professions as they go along. What they need is to enter into the experience of the artist, to move from their existing state of aesthetic awareness, which is often minimal, to deeper levels of insight, intuition, and appreciation which can only come from learning to see, to hear, to feel, to experience in the way artists do.

Since they do not find this in the content of their college education, they are therefore turning to their own culture and its resources for the enjoyment of art forms and kinds of aesthetic experience unavailable inside the educational system. As a result, the schools and colleges have lost touch with their own students and have fallen behind the culture, while a new youth culture with its own style, its own tastes, and its own cultural heroes is thriving outside the academies.

I am not suggesting that the youth culture and its art objects be transplanted into the college curriculum and substituted for what is now there in the collected cultures of the past and present. I mean that the capacity in students to respond to the arts of poetry, music, dance, theater, photography, films, painting, and sculpture has already been developed by the mass culture, and it is up to the colleges and universities to build on that capacity by making the practice of the arts a basic part of the students' educational experience.

Some of the ways in which this can be done through the transformation of the university English department into a center for the literary arts are described later on in this book. The main point there is to invite the students to express themselves in all the forms of the spoken and written word—poetry, drama, story-telling, film and ballet scenarios, radio and television scripts, documentary reports—and to make this an integral part of the study of the works of writers, poets, critics, novelists, literary historians, and others who have a place in the history of past and present literature. Other ways exist in a transformation of the work going on in humanities courses in general, once the emphasis is shifted from dealing with the arts at second hand by talking about them, to learning what they mean by practicing them.

This would involve collaboration with the existing departments in the arts, possibly through double appointments, in which courses offered in the humanities division could be taught by dancers, painters, or theater directors, with practical experience in dance, theater and the other arts arranged as a form of field work for the course. The difference between students enrolled as majors in the departments and schools of the arts and students who are including the arts as part of the B.A.

degree is merely one of emphasis. Students who intend to go on professionally will obviously spend time in the full details of theater, dance, and music productions; the general student will act, draw, dance, sing, compose, in a less demanding schedule, using the whole campus as a studio, theater and auditorium rather than the particular buildings that house the regular arts programs.

It should also be possible to break down the distinction between those who work in the arts because they want to and those who want to and intend to become professionals. This is a good place to apply the philosophy of student teaching which this book advocates, and to draw into the general courses as teachers the students who have shown their talents as musicians, dancers, composers, actors, and artists of all kinds. The departments in the arts or the colleges and divisions of fine arts already have students enrolled who either do not intend going into the professional fields or else—and this is more serious—will not be able to because there are no posts to be filled. Too often the departments and divisions in the arts are so committed to professional training that the educational purpose of releasing the students into new modes of thought and expression, or, to put it more formally, using the arts as a mode of liberal education, is lost in the shuffle.

The work in theater, dance, and music in such cases becomes so much a matter of putting on performances and competing for parts and a chance to perform in productions that the simpler kinds of work—informal workshops and experiments which no one sees except the participants and a few friends, pieces of dialogue, short compositions in dance, poetry and music—are subordinate to full length plays and concerts confined to the very best of the performers. That is of course necessary as part of the work of the universities in giving a home to the arts where new creative talent can be developed, but the concept is vulnerable to the same criticism as the professionalism of sports on the campuses, where most of the money, time, and attention goes to those few performers who play the games for spectators, while the rest of the student body has only a minimal chance to enjoy the sports as participants.

Much can be done to extend the influence of the departments and divisions of the arts into the student body at large, with an array of courses designed for the nonprofessional student. A great deal of the field work in art for the general humanities courses could be arranged by the students themselves with help from the arts students, following the general pattern described in the previous chapter on the reorganization of the lecture system.

That is, one full class meeting a week organized by the faculty leader and a student steering committee, if the leader wants one, with individual and group projects in the arts worked out by students and the leader, in a schedule which replaces the three discussion groups, seminars and research each week in the general pattern. In the case of the visual arts, since there will not be enough room in the studios for everyone to paint and sculpt in the conventional media, drawings, paintings, collages, photography, work in cardboard sculpture, electronics, string, paper, and other materials could be carried out wherever there is space in dormitory rooms, on wooden fences covered with butcher paper, in empty evening classrooms, in cooperative boarding houses where whole interiors could be transformed.

The teaching schedule over the semester could vary from intensive work in a medium for three weeks followed by two or three weeks of other work combined with discussion classes on topics raised in the previous three weeks, to an intensive reading period, visits to museums, the preparation of slides, review of art books, or study in the history of dance. Naturally the field work would make use of the rehearsals and performances of local theater, dance and music groups, and students from the school of fine arts would be recruited for help in the teaching and in student workshops.

On many campuses informal arrangements of a kind which make many of these things possible are already in existence. What is missing is a university point of view which assigns a place to education through art. Some of what is missing will inevitably be restored by what the students themselves do, some of it through their experimental colleges. But even here, few such colleges in the past have included new courses in the arts among the offerings. It should be possible to experiment with two-year internal colleges built on the model of Black Mountain, where the arts provided the basis for an educational program which included other subjects, chosen as these met the interests of the students, and where the teachers and the students were free to invent their own curriculum as they went along. "Every evening you came to dinner," said the late poet Charles Olson who was rector during the period before Black Mountain closed, "and you never knew what was going to happen—a concert, a show, a dance, a reading. I'd never heard of David Tudor, but suddenly there was a concert by a pianist named David Tudor on a Sunday afternoon. . . ."

The Black Mountain teachers were all practitioners in the arts, humanities and sciences who joined the college because they were interested in inventing new art forms and new forms of education. In the vintage years around 1948 a group of comparative unknowns that included John Cage, Merce Cunningham, Willem de Kooning, David Tudor, and Robert Rauschenberg as well as Josef Albers, worked with students at some of the ideas for multi-media art works and happenings which have now come into the main stream of the history of the arts, as has the work of the Black Mountain poets led by Charles Olson himself.

All that is required to start such experimental colleges inside, or in cooperation with, the universities, is to appoint a faculty, assemble a student body and turn them loose for a one-or-two-year program, with full credit toward the B.A. degree for those who meet the standards of work agreed upon by the college. Although every college of this kind might not produce the results of Black Mountain through its twenty-three years, there should be a home on every campus for education through art, without confining the arts to any of the professional schools.

I saw a small example of how this might work in improving the general atmosphere of a campus at San Diego State College in California last year, where the students, through the student government, organized what they called an Education Circus for a week, with young activists and educational reformers brought from outside the campus to see what could be done to make the life of the college more interesting, at least for the week. One part of the program involved recess, in which the San Diego students were invited to play games together outdoors—hop scotch, jump rope, kick the ball, and anything else they thought of—along with invitations to work on disposable sculpture made from cardboard, straw, feathers, string, pieces of wood, or anything else that was handy and could be used, as well as painting and sign-making on sheets of brown paper tacked to a nearby construction fence.

At a college or university which took the arts as a celebration of life on the campus there would be days and weeks of this kind all year, with noon-hour happenings, dancing on the grass, parades with costumes, picnics with poetry readings, street theater, comedians, orchestras, experiments with jazz whistles, guitars, kazoos, washboards and suitcases, banners, posters, songs, choruses, chanting, children's fairs, all in the spirit of celebration of the arts of living, all of it evanescent, serious in its intent to bring art into life, liberating in the way it can give full rein to fantasy.

Bring in the engineering students to invent new art forms with design students, painters to join up with actors to create new environments. Assume that in every person there is an artist struggling to get out, and turn the courses in the arts and humanities into enterprises for releasing ideas and expressions which otherwise the world would never see. Once the spirit of free expression in the arts is generated on the campus by simple and honest displays of wit, imagination, and fantasy, the intellectual and aesthetic temperature is raised and the educational climate changes.

13. The Department as a Learning Center

Reconstruct the Departmental System So That Each Department Becomes a Study and Learning Center for Students.

I hesitate to say it one more time, but the departmental system is another administrative convenience in that total set of administrative conveniences that is the university. The department is the creature of the academic profession and provides the locus for academic careers. It breeds and chooses its own kind of specialists in subject matter according to the inbred specifications of the specialists already in the departments. Although the regular departmental budget is determined mainly by the number of students enrolled in the subject, and it is therefore the students' and the taxpayers' money the departments are spending, in only rare cases do departments set as their first requirement for membership a proven ability to teach. They look first for research credentials and publications and many of the members perish as teachers by publishing.

Yet the system of instruction is centered in the departments and the point of view about what a university is, does and should do is decided in the departments. I have attended more curriculum committees than I care to count in which the content of the discussion about the curriculum had to do exclusively with how many credits of what subjects from given departments should be required of all the students. That was the extent of the educational discussion. Without the requirements the departments would be unprotected from student desertion and would suffer loss of numbers and therefore loss of prestige and power. I have also attended department meetings where teaching assignments were handed around, with the large freshman and introductory courses given to the least experienced instructors, and seniority of faculty rank deciding how little teaching a professor was asked to do.

In earlier years, fresh from my experience at the University of Wisconsin and Sarah Lawrence College (where there are no formal departments), I used to call for abolishing departments and substituting general divisions and groupings of faculty members from various fields according to their intellectual and educational interests. I have given that up as a quixotic gesture, and I see very little chance of doing away with the departmental system. It is unlikely that the departments will vote themselves out of existence, and the power of deans and presidents in relation to the departments has been greatly reduced since the days when Robert Hutchins was able by sheer force of will and administrative talent to reorganize the University of Chicago.

One of the most familiar reasons the departments over the years have become the restricted preserve of the academic professionals is that the subjects of their research have necessarily become more specialized. In the brief period of the past seventy-five years, what used to be called natural and moral philosophy, an over-all name for the social sciences and the humanities, has been subdivided into special fields with subdivisions within them, while science, also a branch of natural philosophy, has manufactured its own variations and special corners. We may be coming around the corner again when we think of what is now done in the name of psychiatry, sociology, and anthropology in the research of Erik Erikson, C. Wright Mills, Margaret Mead, and Noam Chomsky, whose work may be classified under the heading of natural and social philosophy.

Another reason for the impracticality of the departments as teaching instruments is that the models they have taken for the way they have organized themselves are drawn from the bureaucracies, and they have become corporations and guilds, agencies of subject matter rather than communities of people with common interests in ideas. This has had the effect of narrowing the range of interests of the academic specialists and their students rather than broadening them, with most of the preparation of the departmental members for their posts taking place in the one-dimensional world of the academy rather than in the total environment of the world of social, cultural and political phenomena. It has also had the effect of making the research findings of the academies irrelevant both to the education of their students and to the problems now racking our society.

There are ways of making a teaching strength out of what is now a weakness. Instead of retaining departments built around the academic qualifications and research interests of the faculty, convert them into study and learning centers for students. Consider them as internal colleges on their own, where students interested in the general subjects taught by the department are invited to work with the faculty in research, in the invention of new courses and in the advancement of their own knowledge in the field dealt with by the department. Use the departments as the base for double appointments of faculty members who spend half their teaching time in the department and the other half in different kinds of experimental programs of teaching with students and faculty members from other departments. Invite the freshmen and sophomores to join the departments according to their interest, as if they were entering their own college. There would be no danger of over-specialization for the students if the courses were planned as ways of exploring the fields rather than as specializing in them, and if, from their base in the departments, the students were free to move widely through the other parts of the university curriculum.

The departments are already autonomous small colleges with their own faculty members, sometimes eighty to one hundred of them, with their own graduate students and their own policies. The professional life of the university faculty member is lived there and not in the university as a whole. That is one of the weaknesses in the present arrangement. There is too little sense of colleagueship across departmental lines, especially in teaching. Although there is always some talk of inter-disciplinary cooperation and sometimes there are courses taught by two or three representatives of different disciplines, a man's home is in his department and his career and interests lie within his discipline. As far as teaching and the curriculum are concerned, he is interested in the place of his discipline in the educational scheme, and he wants to make his contribution to the teaching program as an expert in his own field.

Since that is the fact and will remain the fact, one solution is to make the teaching reforms inside the departments without trying to convert the university across the board into a different kind of teaching institution. Once you convert the departments you have converted the university. All that is necessary to make the conversion from a department to a study and learning center is an enterprising chairman who is seriously interested in education and in students, and enough volunteer departmental members to make up the manpower for the center.

It is not even necessary to change the name of the department; it can go on being called a department, except that it has a more spacious conception of its place in the university. It is a research and learning institute for students, a place for them to feel at home, a base for them inside the fragmented university. They come to that departmental center because they want to join, and they are made welcome, not simply because they have to take the required courses. Once they get there, they can help make up their own. They don't have to become specialists in the academic sense. They can do as much work in the departmental field as seems appropriate to their total education and the rest of it can be done elsewhere, on and off the campus.

What I am looking for in this conception of a department is a place for students to be, to start from and come back to, a place where faculty members feel free to work with students in their own way, an operating center from which teaching and learning experiments can come on a regular and continuing basis. At the present time it is unlikely that any university will have more than a handful of faculty members who are seriously interested in reforming the entire teaching system, and except in the internal or cluster colleges that have been formed inside the big university, or in the faculty committees on educational development, there is no solid operating base for educational change.

A new conception of the department would give the university this base. In the present system there is already a great deal of room for individual teachers in the departments to teach in their own styles, with whatever reforms in content and method they want to try. Most departmental chairmen and curriculum bodies are happy to encourage faculty members who are willing to make the extra effort to teach experimental courses, and some of the best ideas for improving the teaching have come from this kind of individual experiment. What they are much less willing or able to do is to alter the teaching budget to spend more money on new programs, and most all-university programs for improvement involve more money. In fact some faculty members and administrators assume that it is impossible to change anything without a foundation grant or a project supported by the federal government.

One of the simplest ways of changing the style and content of learning in the present departmental system is to take the present course titles and invent new courses under their names. Most of the courses have numbers, the beginning courses are called Introductory. Keep the numbers, keep the titles, rearrange the content, design a new learning program.

As the system now works, it is much harder to install a new course than to construct a new one under an old title. New courses have to be approved by a departmental committee and chairman, usually by a faculty curriculum committee, by a dean, and sometimes by a vice president for academic affairs. Old courses go on and on. They are seldom taken out of the curriculum, seldom reconstructed, and seldom reviewed for the purpose of deciding whether or not they have outlived their usefulness. Since this is the case, why not encourage those who are interested in extending the range of educational experiment to see what can be done without having to go through all the adjudicating bodies which block the way to action and invention?

There is no reason why, within the present structure and budget, three or four faculty members from a group of departments, retaining the existing faculty-student ratio, should not be given responsibility for three or four hundred freshmen or sophomores for the whole of their work in a given semester and be invited to see what they could do to invent a new kind of learning environment for all of them. This would eliminate two of the present problems—the lack of relationship between one course and another in the freshman and sophomore years, and the lack of opportunity for the members of departments to work with each other in making new curricula which are not tied to the regular departmental requirements.

The program of the integrated curriculum at the University of Wisconsin is a case in point. There faculty members from four departments built a four-course, two-year program of inter-related studies as an alternative to the regular curriculum. There is no special reason why every freshman and every sophomore should be asked to go through identical programs in the five-course spread, and experience with two-year curricula which break from the regular system—the Meiklejohn experiment in the 1920's and 1930's at the University of Wisconsin was one of the first and best known examples—shows that there is no need for identical subject matter covered by all students as preparation for their third year. It is more a question of the degree of involvement of the students in an internal community of their own, and the quality of learning available there through the interests of the teachers. The main thing is that students learn how to be students and learn how to learn, how to use the resources of the university through the work they do at a center within it. They are more likely to be able to do this, and at the same time prepare themselves for their continuing education if they *belong* somewhere, even if it is only to a department willing to sponsor them, or to three or four faculty members with whom they can identify.

Arrangements of this sort have already been made at the University of California in Los Angeles, where the problems of the mass university have involved the students, faculty and administration in work together without the hostilities and confrontations of Berkeley and elsewhere. Starting in 1966 with a two-day Conference on Undergraduate Education with all three sections of the university represented equally, the planning for change has moved ahead faster than in most other institutions, with the help of a student experimental college, and in this case, what could be easily duplicated elsewhere, a variation of the student experimental college idea called the Committee for the Study of Education and Society. The Committee was organized spontaneously without going through months of meetings and faculty legislation, by a professor of physics and the dean of graduate studies who both felt that the student demands for relevance and a full share of responsibility in curriculum-making

were justified. Their idea was to sponsor new courses and
seminars for credit in studying "the current social problems of our society," and to bring in interested faculty
members and students from any part of the university to
work out courses together. The difference between this
and a student experimental college is that the central idea
remains the same but the initiative come from the faculty
and administration who join with the students as colleagues.

In addition the University has a faculty Committee on
Educational Development to approve courses initiated by
students and faculty, and an Institute for the Study of
American Cultures. It is this Institute which comes clos-
est to the idea of converting departments into centers,
since its members remain as departmental members and
offer courses and research with colleagues from other
departments. Under the Institute plan, there are four
centers, Afro-American History and Culture, Mexican-
American History and Culture, Oriental-American History and Culture, and American Indian Research. The
centers have given the students a full chance to work as
equals with the faculty in planning the programs and
courses, and students are members with equal standing in
the steering committees now making present and future
policy for each center.

The virtue of the UCLA Institute is the one I have been
looking for in the idea of reconstructing the departmental
concept—it does not have to fight the departments in order to exist. It leaves them intact but uses their resources
for innovation and change both in the content and methods of the curriculum, and it invites the students into a
genuine educational partnership. In some institutions
the organization of an institute with centers developed
within it may be the best way to deal with the immediate
problems of organizing for change, although one draw-
back for universities in general is that it adds an addi-

tional administrative structure and would be hard to operate on a university-wide scale once it went past the new work in the social sciences and the humanities.

But the main point is that the UCLA arrangements have sprung from the initiative of faculty members from the departments with the strong support of the administration, as far as long-run change is concerned, there is much more leverage in this approach than in any other. Once the departments and their individual members begin to make the reforms, the ideas spread from there to the university at large. With an increase in the number of students who have had some experience in unstandardized learning, the sophistication of the student body about educational reform increases, and more teachers are asked to deal directly with student interests and needs as they actually exist—in the day-to-day teaching and learning through which the students go. Each department, according to its willingness and interest, could sponsor its own student experimental college and student research center as a part of its regular program.

As I have already pointed out, a great deal of the frustration of students about their education lies in the fact that all the time and energy going into the student-faculty committees on educational reform does not affect their own education at all. That simply goes along in the same way as before while all the studies are being made.

If a department and its chairman wished to tackle these problems directly, things could begin happening the next day, the next week, at any point in the college year and at any point in the curriculum, junior and senior students who had become majors in the department could be invited to join in teaching in some of the ways I have described—as teaching assistants, tutors, discussion leaders, and advisers, among other things. There could be an advisory group of the majors elected from among themselves or appointed by the chairman of the department to serve as an educational policies committee for the development of courses and ideas in cooperation with the faculty.*

Graduate students in the department would have their own educational policies committee to work on questions of curriculum, graduate study, degree requirements, and the relation of graduate students to undergraduate teaching. One of the places where the graduate students could give the most help would be in reorganizing the way in which their talents as teachers are now used.** As part of their work toward the graduate degree, they should have a full chance to teach courses of their own, provided they can show that they have the talent for it. As of now, whatever teaching they do is so closely linked to the lecture-test-credit-grade system that they are little more than graders and examination readers. If they are critics of the system, as more and more of them are, they are frustrated by the role they are forced to play as assistants to professors who lecture. Since most of them are going to be teachers either in college or in high school, the sooner they are given a chance to take responsibility as teachers, the better for their education, and, if they are chosen with care, the better for the education of the undergraduates with whom they work.

Under the plan for student learning centers, graduate students teaching groups of undergraduates would be under the supervision of an experienced member of the department who would be responsible for their appointment and would organize a seminar in education and teaching to meet weekly and would deal with general issues in education and university affairs as well as specific

* This idea has already been discussed across the country and in some cases put into practice, as in the graduate work in sociology at Columbia. The idea also appears in the Foote Report on University Governance at the University of California in Berkeley.
** The Graduate Students Union movement has already included negotiations on this and related issues in its bargaining with the universities.

questions the graduate students raised from the experience of teaching their own classes. The semester of teaching and seminar would receive full credit toward the graduate degree, and the seminar would be the only course work of the student during that term of his teaching. If the student were already receiving a graduate scholarship or fellowship, his teaching would be subsidized by it; if not, he would be given a stipend. The question of the total reform of the requirements for the Ph.D. could be left in abeyance for further experiment and analysis. In the meantime a reform would have been made in the Ph.D. program by the simple device of including in it the semester of teaching and learning about education and about the subject matter of the student's own field.

14. An Example from New Mexico

I had a chance to try out some of these ideas with graduate students while teaching at the University of New Mexico during six weeks of a seminar there in 1970. The course was not planned as a seminar in teaching. It turned out to be partly that because six of the students in it *were* teaching, one of them in an elementary school, the others as graduate assistants in the English and American studies departments.

The course was entitled The Radical Transformation of the University, its sixteen students, drawn from the university as a whole but mainly from the social sciences and humanities, came from fourteen different universities, from California to Virginia, and represented every kind of undergraduate background imaginable. My purpose in the seminar was to take up the main questions which had been bothering me about the university and its relation to politics, society, social and educational change, and the student revolt, to see what could be done in an experimental course to develop answers from the students to some of the questions.

We met once a week for three hours. I asked the students to meet in pairs or in small groups among themselves as often as they could during the rest of the week at times convenient to themselves. I kept daily blocks of time for office hours, both on the campus and in my apartment during a few evenings. There were no examinations, no grades, and no assignments other than a written educational autobiography from each at the beginning, and projects we worked out together after each student had had a chance to do some reading and thinking about what issue, topic, or problem he wanted to deal with. I later provided a list of fifteen such possible projects.

Only one of the students had ever worked before in an

140

open teaching situation of this kind. In the beginning the students found it hard, without specific assignments and an examination and grade to work toward, to know what was expected of them. They were not used to making their own appointments in a professor's office, and they did not realize that with as many open office hours during the day and evening, they were free to come in at any time to talk about whatever they had on their minds. During the first week only four of them came. I had given the class a preliminary bibliography of around forty items, books which dealt with the student protest movement, university reform, and educational philosophy, ranging from my own work to Jencks and Riesman's *The Academic Revolution* and Jerry Avorn's *Up Against the Ivy Wall*. I expected that, as graduate students, they would choose their own items from the bibliography and begin their own reading in preparation for choosing a project.

That did not turn out to be the case, and I then became much more explicit about what I wanted them to do. Each of the educational autobiographies was mimeographed and distributed, giving us original material which we used to discuss the education they had received and were receiving, the major influences on their lives from teachers, parents, other persons, and the society itself.

One student, a very interesting poet, did not like the idea of writing a personal statement for others to read, and wrote out instead a set of quotations from writers he admired, saying that this would tell the others more about him than anything he could write himself. Another student used his autobiography to make an attack on the social system after saying about himself only that he had attended school and learned very little. It was a free form of expression and it unleashed ideas which many of the students had not thought about before because they had never compared notes on their lives in school and college. On the basis of what they learned about each other they began meeting in pairs or in groups at other times in the week, and included my office as one of the places they met when they had something to talk about in which they wanted to get me involved. They also began bringing ideas, articles, short pieces of their own writing to class and to me, to be included in work we were doing together.

A student who was teaching in an elementary school became interested in the problems of change in the public school system, and joined forces with another student who had had experience teaching in a community college, to analyze the role of parents in influencing educational policy. Both of them knew at first hand the restrictions placed on public school teachers in the content and methods of their teaching, and added personal testimony to the discussion of problems of academic freedom, community involvement in the schools, and the control of the curriculum by political forces.

At that time the University of New Mexico had been heavily criticized by members of the state legislature, among others, for having defended a young black instructor who had introduced an obscene poem into the reading for an English course. One of the legislators, as a service to the state, had distributed fifty thousand copies of the poem around the state to show the citizens how the university was corrupting the minds of the students, and a fair amount of agitation was produced by citizens who wanted to protect the students after having withstood the corruption themselves. A committee of the legislature had been formed to investigate the university and to recommend legislation to control its poetry and its radicals, with the university as a target for citizens' anger against student demonstrations.

I asked for volunteers from the class to study the political relations of the university and the state, and to interview the legislators who were most hostile to the university. That became the first project, and three of the students made the study of politics and education their major topic throughout the term, producing brief reports

on the situation in New Mexico for the benefit of the class
as we went along.

Other students worked on the topic of the communes,
of which there are a good many near Albuquerque and
Taos, as examples of a new kind of learning and living
center with implications for the reform of university residential arrangements. Others worked on the grading system, the use of federal funds for university research, and
a range of other topics which were not only of national
concern among educators, but which were actual issues
affecting the University of New Mexico. As the usual incidents of student disruption and protest occurred—interference with a basketball game with Brigham Young
University, disruption of a speech by Strom Thurmond,
demands by the Chicano students for a budget from the
Associated Students. They were discussed and studied
by the class, some of whose members volunteered to collect information about similar incidents on other campuses.

I also dealt with some of the major policy questions in
social and educational philosophy in a series of all-university public lectures and at meetings called by various
groups, including one called by the faculty entitled "How
to Save the University." My students attended these and
brought to class their comments on the attitudes and questions of the audience as well as on the content of my remarks and those of other faculty members and students.

Other members of the faculty and other students not
in the seminar began to visit the weekly sessions, some of
them bringing in articles they had written, essays they
had read, and information from other colleges and
schools. Some of the visitors struck up friendships with
the seminar members, at times helped with research the
members were doing, invited them to visit other classes
in which they were enrolled.

Student research on university policy and educational
philosophy provided the main body of material for the

work of the class, and the students who were teaching
began to speculate about how they could apply some of
the ideas proposed in class to the reform of their own
teaching in the courses to which they had been assigned.
They found that when they tried to apply similar methods
in their own classes there was resistance from their students who were nervous about leaving the conventional
ways and could see that the new ways would involve them
in spending more time in the course than they felt they
could afford.

Through that kind of experience with their own students my students learned a great deal about themselves,
both as students and as teachers, and many things which
I was concerned to teach them about different styles of
learning they learned on their own. One student who had
missed the opening session and had not found time to
come in to talk about the course during the first week
gave the class a speech at the second session about the
evils of grading and declared that the present course was
an example of how hypocritical progressives were since
they talked one way and taught another. He ended with
a call to the other members of the class to vote unani-
mously that everyone would receive an A at the end of the
term.

I kept silent while the other members of the class explained to the newcomer that this was a course without
grades and that it was just as foolish to vote everyone an
A as it was to award any of the other letters. Later on,
after I had left the course in the hands of a colleague who
was conducting the seminar with me, the student denounced my teaching, in an article in the student newspaper, on the grounds that it claimed to be open and free
but that it actually involved my leading discussions and
making assignments, and therefore betrayed the theory
and practices I was proposing. Other students replied by
discussing the problem of discussion, the best use of a

teacher's time, and how to protect themselves from long-winded discussants.

I found reluctance on the part of some of the students to do much reading, either in my books or in the work of the authors in the bibliography. When we discussed this in class and in conference, three facts turned up. (1) The non-readers assumed that they were going to hear my views in class and that the reading would therefore be redundant (they quoted back to me my view that more was learned by student writing and research than by spending all the time reading) to which I responded by saying that I didn't intend to take up valuable class time by the repetition of my own views when these were easily available in the books and articles I had written. (2) The library system was such that getting a book for a period long enough to do much with it was very hard indeed and that the library services discouraged anyone from trying. This resulted in a study of the library services by one of the students and an inquiry into the relation of books and reading assignments to education in general. The general conclusion, based on the students' experience with their undergraduate education as well as with the University of New Mexico, was that university libraries and book stores were obstacles rather than aids to student reading. (3) Graduate students had so much reading to do (the whole of their education was conducted through reading assignments and papers based on them) that those who were teaching courses of their own while carrying a full set of graduate courses had no time for their own education. The answer to that, it seemed to us, would be to free the student who was himself teaching, from all but one other course, counting his teaching as a fundamental part of his work toward a higher degree, on the grounds that graduate students learned more by teaching than they could by taking courses.

A mythology has developed about the reasons for this generation of students being uninterested in reading and being profoundly anti-print, with McLuhanesque reasoning to account for it. When one moves beneath the surface of the myths, it usually turns out that it is availability rather than anti-printism that decides on the interest in reading. Although it is perfectly true, thank God, that this generation is interested in film, tape, electronic devices, and mixed media of communication of all kinds, and that students turn to them naturally, it is also true that they, especially the undergraduates and their teachers, have not yet learned to use the full range of paperbacks and xerography as instruments for their own work. It is still an unnatural act to buy a book of one's own which is not a required textbook to be sold immediately after the course is over. In case after case, in my own experience, the books needed at a specific time for specific purposes on the campuses are simply not available in either the college or the local book stores, in paperback or any other form. That and the fact that students are used to spending three to five dollars for a rock concert or a movie, and can't find a dollar for a paperback indicate a problem for practical education, not necessarily for Marshall McLuhan.

During the work we did together in the seminar, many lessons were learned all around, and it seemed to me that if graduate students had more chance to work in the ways the educational reformers propose, with central seminars of the kind with which we experimented, the ideas could begin to be tested on a much wider scale, both by the students and the faculty. All that this sort of experiment requires from the department is the services of faculty members interested in university reform as well as in the subject matter of their own discipline. In the case of the Transformation of the University course, when the May strike came to the New Mexico campus, several members of the class who had already been studying the free university movement combined forces to start a free university in place of the regular classes; my teaching colleague in the course served as chairman of the coordinating committee.

I cite this small example of the departmental idea in action to indicate the network of relationships which can spring up once there are centers in the departments and in the faculty for experiments in change. Two other examples from New Mexico are relevant. Over a year ago, by faculty action, a new degree was approved, the Bachelor of University Studies, which differed from the regular degree in the fact that it involved no subject matter requirements for graduation. The faculty action was taken in response to the fact that a number of students who had done well enough in their courses throughout the first three or four years to be recognized as good students had not completed the requirements and although they had a sufficient number of credits to graduate, could not do so under the current system.*

At the same time, in response to another set of needs, a program of undergraduate seminars had been installed by faculty vote, by which any faculty member, from whatever department, who wished to volunteer to teach a new non-departmental course of his own choosing on a topic of interest to students, could do so, with the credit counting toward graduation and the teaching counted in the faculty member's teaching schedule. The program also arranged that any group of students or individual student with ideas for a new course could start an undergraduate seminar provided a faculty member agreed to teach it.

Although it had not been planned that way, the university had inadvertently made for itself an instrument of

* Through the initiative of the dean of the College of Fine Arts at the University of New Mexico, an invitation in the form of a brief brochure was issued to all the students in the college to prepare a proposed curriculum for themselves for the years toward graduation with reasons for their proposals. Approximately one third of the students took advantage of the chance to choose their own program, the rest preferred to stay with the regular courses and requirements.

reform and change which could have serious consequences in meeting many of the defects in the present system, without having to wait for a mandate from the faculty as a whole for a complete change in university policy. The departments had been left intact, but room had been given for the development of many different kinds of change, depending only on the imagination and initiative of students and faculty members working together. If the program of undergraduate seminars were expanded to include the development of new courses on a broader scale, with cooperation from the departments in sponsoring internal arrangements comparable to those of the undergraduate seminars, the departments could be the agents of change so badly needed in the present university system.

The situation at the University of New Mexico is one of openness to change once initiatives are taken by students and faculty members. In fact, the New Mexico example is more typical of the situation for reform in most universities than are the more celebrated instances of confrontations and disruptions over the introduction of Black Studies, open enrollment or any of the other issues which have involved the campuses in sustained and therefore dangerous dissension. The Chicano students at the University of New Mexico organized their own program for a Chicano center, received help and support from the president, the vice president for academic affairs and the faculty in putting it together. By using existing courses among the departmental offerings with a shift in some of the content, plus some new ones, along with a tutorial and counselling program of Chicano juniors and seniors for the freshmen and for high school students interested in applying for university admission, the students found that they could build on what already existed without the necessity of attacking the university for its lack of initiative in the past.

On its part, the university found the initiative of the

students the most important source of ideas and energies
for developing a very important and neglected part of the
university curriculum. The black students on the campus
produced a comparable program of their own, established
a Black Studies center and a set of courses and activities
to go with it, as did the American Indian students. The
main limitation on the amount that could be done in these
three basic areas of educational change was financial; it
did not lie in any obstacles put in the way of change either
by the faculty or the administration.

As for other changes, there is no need to wait in any
university for the students to organize themselves, either
to confront the university or to install their own student
programs. A single departmental chairman willing to
take on the responsibility of being an educator as well as
a scholar and teacher, can put together a group of members who feel the same way and are willing to spend time
and energy on the innovations. Even in the absence of a
group of such people, a chairman who looks toward the
future can begin recruiting and can work directly with
some of the activist graduate students who are already
teaching assistants and who want to move things forward.
There are already pressures in new directions from the
radical caucuses which have sprung up in each of the
professional associations, and some departments have
their own home-grown radical caucuses among the
younger faculty who are not only ready to move, but are
utterly determined to do so. What is needed now is a
union of faculty and students joined together with a sense
of common purpose.

One major advantage of this shift in the concept of the
department is that it does not seriously disturb the university structure of authority, at least at the beginning,
and puts the reform ideas to a series of tests in practice
where they can stand or fall by their own merits, in the
way the TVA demonstrations influenced the farmers.

Nor does it seriously disturb the departmental members who do not wish to play; most faculty members condone the efforts of others to improve the teaching, provided they are not compelled to fit into a new program which they do not like. Those who, for whatever reason, prefer to go on with a pattern of conventional lecture-credit courses are free to do so. It is even possible that some of them will become infected by the spirit of reform once their colleagues demonstrate, in action, the possibilities of a freer system. In any case, there will always be room for good teachers in any department, no matter what their teaching style.

In saying that this approach does not disturb the present structure of authority, I do not mean to retreat from the front edge of radical reform, but only to say that a head-on assault on the system is not at this point the only way to change it. What I have in mind is to use to the full the possibilities in existing situations, and, using the present authority structure as a base, to welcome the initiatives of students and faculty members with the help, rather than the hindrance, of that authority. Since the line of authority runs from the department and its chairman to the deans to the vice presidents and president, the inclusion of students and non-tenured faculty in the decision-making right at the center of the teaching program is the most immediate way of legitimizing change, while giving the students instant access to a better education.

15. The Spoken and the Written Word: What to Do with the English Department

Suppose that an English department and its chairman were to adopt the idea of serving as a center for the arts of language and literature rather than as a conventional department organized to handle the proper sequences of periods, literary forms, and coverage of literary ground in chronological or other order. A department of this kind would deal with the use of words in speaking and writing, taking for granted the fact that no matter how great a shift within the younger generation and the total culture there is in the direction of films, tapes, theater, mixed media, electronic imagery and information storage, the spoken and the written word remains the basic medium of communication among all of them.

It is the basic medium because the formation of words is so intimately related to the formation of ideas and concepts, and although it is possible to live a rich life of imagery and talk and experience without the use of written words, the word itself is what matters. Most students do not see the connection between speaking and writing, nor between the quality of their own thinking and feeling and the words they use to express it. They have been taught to separate the two the moment they are taught to read, and massive reading problems have been created because reading and writing have been treated as technical skills rather than as natural extensions of speaking and thinking.

This fundamental mistake has been preserved in its primitive form by the structure of the English department. Aside from the traditional freshman English course

151

or English composition, which are courses in learning to
read and write, and therefore to think, the rest of the
course offerings are usually built on the assumption that
books convey information and that they are to be read
for the information they contain and the interpretations
of that information given by experts in English literature.

The English department should never have been allowed to think of English as a subject. The language is
not a subject. It is the means by which rational thought
becomes possible, the basic ingredient in the development
of the child's capacity to think and to feel, the way in
which the human being grows in his understanding of
himself and in his relations with others. There are of
course many languages, signs and symbols—the language
of dance, mathematics, chemistry, sculpture, sex, body
movement, costume. One of the greatest contributions of
the McLuhan argument about the relation of visual imagery to literate cultures is the explosion of the idea that
ideas and values must be conveyed in written form or
not be fully conveyed at all.

But the argument does not go deep enough to the question of how imagery locates itself in concepts related to
the words which identify them. After you have agreed
to the primacy and intensity of a reality transformed by
films and television into new versions of truth and non-
truth, you are still left with the primacy of words as the
means through which the reality itself is understood and
explained.

No matter how loosely organized, there are scenarios
for films, scripts for radio and television programs,
scenarios for ballets and mixed-media happenings, questions for computers, just as in even the wildest of im-
provisations in chance music and avant-garde jazz, there
are head arrangements, whether or not anything is written down. At a given point, someone either has to write
something down, say something, or do something, no

matter what else is happening, just as in the visual arts, at some point there must be a visual object, even if it is only a fragment of flashing light or a junk pile. Once it has happened, it can be described. Even if the art form contains no words at all, there are images and symbols, and these can be and are constantly talked and written about, otherwise there would be no continuity between one aesthetic episode and another, only a discrete set of psychic events. In the matter of happenings, for example, there are a great many more words written about them than there are happenings.

The difference between a regular English department and a center, or between any other regular department and a center, is that rather than working with the regular academic subject matter of a given discipline, the center is designed to deal with the problems and the issues to which the discipline has a contribution to make. A center for the study of politics, or for the study of society, or of the biological sciences, or of the spoken and written word, need not confine itself to sequences of academic courses but can range more widely into the investigation of any phenomenon or idea which seems relevant to the students and faculty members who are attracted to the areas of knowledge dealt with by the departments. The center deals with the education and development of students as a primary rather than peripheral responsibility or as something thrown off as a by-product of the work of the department.

It would be as natural in such a center for the study of politics to carry on work in the politics of peace or the politics of education as it would be in a reconstituted English department to work in the relation between the mass culture and the elites, or the philosophy of contemporary art. A center for philosophical studies would differ from a regular philosophy department by its concern for developing students who could think for themselves on issues affecting the human race, and would use student research, the work of recognized figures in the history of philosophy, faculty research, and joint student-faculty investigations as sources of insight and materials for study. The investigations would be no less rigorous than under the present programs. But they would be carried on with a view to the contribution they made to the growth of the students' capacity for sustained thought and original insight rather than to the reputation for respectability and prestige of the members of the department.

The idea of the center suggests a different model of organization, one that is closer to the art school or the music school or the artists' colony, where the work of the artist and his students is based on a common interest in the creative act and the public demonstration and discussion of a whole variety of aesthetic events. What Gunther Schuller says about himself as a composer-conductor-musician-educator who also writes and teaches can by analogy be transposed into a description of the kind of leadership needed for converting the departments into study and learning centers. In reply to a question about the central purpose in all the activities in which he is involved, Schuller said, "I like the complexity of this kind of life and the way all these activities cross-fertilize. The teaching, the composing, the conducting, the whole educational philosophy—you know, *organizing a school into a fine teaching emporium*—it all draws on my already varied background in a way that I find satisfying. It draws on all the stops that are in me, so to speak." * (Italics mine)

As an administrator responsible for the musical education of six hundred students at the New England Conservatory, Schuller has all the problems of a departmental

* Donal Henahan, *The New York Times*, September 6, 1970. Arts and Leisure section, p. 14.

chairman, a dean, a college president, and a faculty member combined, along with some extra ones involved in his conducting and composing and all the complexities of their inter-relationships. But the complexities are unravelled and knit together again in one major purpose—to contribute his total talent to the enrichment of contemporary culture. That is why Schuller's work in organizing education remains central to his professional life. He works directly with students and finds their talents astonishing, although inhibited by the culture out of which they have come.

"These kids come here," he says of his students at the Conservatory, "some of them, indoctrinated by their school systems to think that only nineteenth-century music is worth anything. But they get the idea here, perhaps in a subliminal way, that contemporary music is their music. They start to relate to it, in spite of their indoctrination. . . . If there is any one emphasis here, it is on the whole idea of ensemble, on training in the realization that you are part of an organism, and why." *

The analogy between Schuller's Conservatory students and those in the colleges breaks down at one point, although it remains a good one. The college student is indoctrinated by the school system to accept conventional academic education as the standard for learning, but he is also indoctrinated by the mass culture, in a subliminal way, to assume that contemporary culture is his culture, and that it is the only one that counts. That presents a different kind of educational problem.

On the other hand, in the concept of the center as a replacement for the department, Schuller's emphasis on the idea of ensemble, on training in the realization that you are part of an organism, is a central operating principle, as is his conception of using a personal body of experience, in his case, as a composer-scholar-conductor,

* Henahan, *ibid.*

to give leadership to his students by the way in which he can help to organize their education. His is a way, as he says, not of training musicians to perfect commercially valuable skills, but to deepen their musical perception. Here the analogy is quite direct.

Another analogy comes to mind in the work and educational philosophy of Allen Ginsberg, who, in his own way, is a one-man traveling English department, with strong educational principles which have had a deep effect on the cultural development of the younger generation. Ginsberg's theory of poetry is close to his theory of education.

> I am sick of preconceived literature [he writes to a friend who is a teacher], and only interested in *writing*, the actual process and technique, wherever it leads, and the various possible experiments in composition that are in my path—and if anybody still is confused in what literature is let it be hereby announced once for all in the 7 Kingdoms that that's what it is—Poetry is what poets write, and not what other people think they should write. . . .

> You've got to have the heart and decency to take people seriously and not depend *only* on your university experience for arbitrary standards of value to judge others by. It doesn't mean that you have to agree that Free Verse is the Only Path to Prosodaic experiment, or that Williams is a Saint, or I have some horrible magic secret. . . .

> Just enough to dig you, to dig what others besides yourself are trying to do, and be interested in their work or not, but not to get in the way, in fact even encourage where you can see some value. And you're in a position to encourage, you teach, you shouldn't hand down limited ideas to younger minds—that was the whole horror of Columbia. . . .

> If you talk fast and excitedly you get weird syntax and rhythms, just like you think, or nearer to what you think. Not that everybody's think process is consciously the same —everybody's got a different consciousness factory—but the attempt here is to let us see—to transcribe the thought all at once so that its ramifications appear on the page.*

* Jane Kramer, *Allen Ginsberg in America* (New York: Random House, 1968), pp. 165–66, 170, 171.

Allen Ginsberg's attitude to teaching and to literature is one which, when adopted, leads to thinking about the way in which formal learning in the arts and sciences could be reorganized to draw upon the internal resources of students rather than exclusively the academic resources of the faculty. As in the case of Schuller, Ginsberg has created his own educational organization and teaching style, through setting up a foundation to help writers, and through sponsoring and planning "be-ins," poetry readings, and literary happenings of all kinds, the difference lying only in the fact that Ginsberg's organization is transitive and mobile and is built around himself as poet-teacher rather than around a department of English.

In the case of more formal and less mobile departments of English, converting them into arts centers means that the teachers would stop "handing down limited ideas to younger minds" and try in every way possible to encourage students to break out of the stereotyped responses they have been taught to make to the standard works of literature and the standard modes of perception in general in all forms of knowledge. The principal period courses and other conventional parts of the curriculum could remain, in deference to the existence and demands of the graduate school and other considerations, but the main thrust of the act of conversion would be in the direction of building a center for the literary arts on the campus, one which would attract students interested in poetry, short stories, novels, plays, film scripts, ballet scenarios, and written work of all kinds. At the moment, the student with a general interest in writing and the arts has nowhere to go, unless he enrolls in a drama department, in dance, music, the visual arts, in speech, or in one of the few writing courses offered in English departments.

Yet there are thousands of students who now come from the high schools with serious literary interests gained from their membership in the youth culture where

they have edited and written for underground newspapers, seen a wide variety of films, read paperbacks,
written poems, followed the movements in rock musicals
and folk art, organized their own high school theater and
music, made their own films, taken a natural interest
in photography. As freshmen they are ready to enter the
next stage of their interests, but can find very little in the
first-or-second-year curriculum which could build on those
interests and deepen their work in the arts in general
and literature in particular.

There are also thousands of other students for whom
an education in literature could mean the entrance into
a world of ideas unavailable anywhere else in the de-
partmentalized curriculum. The purpose in teaching
courses in the humanities and the arts is to educate the
sensibility and to deepen the capacity for aesthetic, social,
and personal insight. If that purpose were taken seriously, it would mean that the English department would
pay a great deal of attention to the idea that language
is the tissue which holds the arts together and makes it
possible to talk about the act of the artist. The art object
exists—poem, painting, sculpture, novel, play—and must
be allowed to say whatever it has to say in its own terms,
to be experienced as itself. But talk about it is unavoid-
able, and the best kind of talk about art is the kind which
the artists carry on among themselves, as tennis players
and football players talk about the game they play.

This would argue for a full opportunity for students
in the English department, with English considered not
as a literary form but as a means of expression in words,
to work directly with dancers, actors, composers, painters, and sculptors, and to write poems to be danced,
stretches of dialogue, scenarios for films, one-act plays,
critiques of art works, through discussions with the student artists who made them. Everything should be done
to encourage the student of literature to become more

deeply involved in the art of expression, and to write and read, especially to write, because he wants to say something and to know something for himself. The more we do of this, the better for the education of his sensibility. This means that he should be writing for his friends, his family, his fellow students, for the university community, not merely for his teacher, who in any case cannot be expected to absorb the thousands and thousands of words which pour out of the thousands of English students and have to be read, marked and returned.

The English department could be the sponsor of poetry festivals, and in collaboration with dancers, choreographers, student playwrights and film-makers, the sponsor of courses and weekend conferences in dance, film, and theater criticism, one of the most neglected areas in the whole of higher education. The English department can—and does, in some cases—establish poetry centers: it could deliberately set out to attract students from everywhere in the country to study English as a first language, and, building on the cultural idiosyncracies and styles of expression among the minority and majority cultures, could create a new culture inside the university, a series of counter-cultures against the prevailing culture of the academy.

In this, a reconstituted English department could combine forces with a psychology department to become in practice a center for the study of human nature. Student research projects linked to joint courses and seminars could deal with original materials developed by the students on a range of topics, including autobiographical studies of the students' own family life, their childhood, their values, comparative studies of psychological attitudes among the poor, the well-to-do, the whites, minority groups, foreign students, the psychology of freedom and authority, the psychological study of peace and war, social disorder, and the attitudes toward education of students, faculty members, administrators, parents, state legislators, clergymen. Collaboration of the same kind could be arranged with a sociology department which could become a center for the study of social institutions; joint courses could be arranged with the English department in the social structure of the college campus, the social history of the American Indian, the Chicanos, the blacks, the first-generation college students.

The emphasis in this kind of collaboration would be on the development of original insight by the students who would be writing on topics to which they had something of their own to bring, with their experience inside American culture providing the material for their writing. It is just one step from student research in psychology and sociology on topics within the area of their own experience to writing short plays, stories, poems, and film scenarios which extend in imagination the content of that experience. We must find the ways in which students can learn to express themselves naturally, without feeling that they must shift gears in order to write a special kind of paper for an English class, another kind for other academic specialties. If they can learn that to write about something is a more precise form of speaking about it and that all writing is a means of finding out what it is you know, we will have helped them on their way to an understanding of the meaning of literature and their own lives.

16. Some Projects Which Will Work

In what follows I have put down a cross-section of examples meant to be illustrative of projects departments could carry out if they adopted the idea of student and learning centers as a working proposition. They are examples of what else might be done; some of them are already going on in college and university programs. But not enough of them and not with enough intensity and variety to make an observable difference in the total university atmosphere.

The Political Science Department: Center for the Study of Politics

Among other things, the political science department could sponsor an undergraduate research center, built around new courses and the work of students in them, where studies and research projects could be carried out in the politics of education, or in political issues in local and state politics, in the relation of the university to the state legislature and the federal government, the politics of the peace movement, government policy in scientific research, or whatever other areas were considered relevant to the political education of students in contemporary America. Joint student research with faculty members on the role of the student movement in politics could be arranged with students from a number of departments. Undergraduate intercollegiate weekend conferences could be arranged to bring students from other campuses to work with the students in the local department on issues in the politics of education, in the politics of the Black Power Movement, or in the politics of the poor. Reports for presentation at the conference could be made on political conditions in the local community from which the visiting students came. Local students could be sent to other campuses for a semester of study and research, especially in the case of majors in political science who are planning their own curricula and have begun their own research projects.

Other Kinds of Study Centers

A psychology, sociology, or economics department could start a Women's Studies program or center of the kind organized in 1970 by twelve women students at San Diego State College who became interested in extending the work of a women's liberation course in which they were enrolled as part of the student experimental college offerings on the campus. Six hundred students signed petitions in support of a Women's Studies program. The twelve students talked to the dean of arts and sciences who was sympathetic to the idea of student initiative in curriculum reform and to their ideas for experiment in the field of women's education. The students then talked to faculty members they knew to be sympathetic, and right away the Women's Studies program was established simply by converting the content of five existing courses in three departments into studies which focused on particular issues in cultural and social history and contemporary society which were of special relevance to women.

From there the idea went to the student council where it was endorsed by a resolution supporting the new curriculum and the idea of a Women's Studies Center, with a physical location on the campus, where offices, a library, duplicating equipment, etc., could be housed. As parts of the center program, the students have planned a Community Center for Women (a storefront in the community for information services on birth control, abortion, counselling, educational services), a Recruitment and Tutorial Center to bring education to women in the community and to provide tutoring in any field in which they are interested, a Day Care Center staffed by men and women students, and Research Publications and Cultural Centers for women in the community and on the campus.

The curriculum part of the program is now in operation with the collaboration of faculty members from the English, sociology, political science, psychology, history, and home economics departments offering twelve courses along with opportunities for student-initiated field work. The courses are all electives, and a student may enroll in the Women's Studies program while still completing a major in a given department. Five faculty members from various departments serve as an advisory committee and make recommendations, in collaboration with the students, to the dean of arts and letters for appointments, retentions, promotions, etc.

As sponsored by a department or group of departments, the freshness and originality of the San Diego experiment by the students could be preserved by inviting interested students from the women's liberation movement and elsewhere on the campus to put together their own ideas for the conversion of existing courses and the addition of new ones. From there the planning and execution could proceed as far as the faculty members and students cared to take it.

Science Fairs and Demonstrations

The idea of the science fair, sponsored by departments, could be used more broadly on the campuses, and projects involving public display and student guides to discuss the exhibits and explain them to visitors could be planned as part of the course work. Students could prepare films and tapes on problems and experiments as part of their course work and could be asked to organize, conduct, and explain experiments for the benefit of other students in other courses. Courses such as Social Implications of Nuclear Energy, taught in the physics department by Professor David Inglis at the University of Massachusetts in Amherst, could be conducted jointly with a sociology or philosophy department, with students from each department organizing their own seminars and discussion groups, and with physics students responsible for helping the sociology and philosophy students with the physics, and vice versa for the physics students in sociology and philosophy.

A variation in this kind of course invention took place in the political science department at Northwestern University where students organized a one-day curriculum fair to which students and faculty brought their own course proposals written out in detail. The main action at the fair was the negotiation of students and teachers for a new curriculum as they sat around tables discussing the proposals.

If a student had in hand a course with a guaranteed enrollment of at least five members and could find a faculty member to head it, the course went into the curriculum for the following quarter. If five or more students were interested in joining any of the courses the faculty brought to the fair, these too went into the curriculum. It would be a simple matter to extend the idea of the fair into a whole variety of curriculum sessions.

Libraries of Student Work

In all the departments, libraries of student work could be started, and student research, creative work in literature, educational materials, film strips, tapes, recordings, videotapes, and course outlines made available to students in the department and elsewhere. These would be usable in other courses, both those initiated by students and those taught by the regular faculty. The advantage in this, aside from making some useful material available to students and teachers, is that there would be somewhere to write for other than a place on a professor's desk already loaded with student papers. The whole idea of student paper-writing can be lifted in this way from

its present status of obligatory credit and grade-getting
to its proper role as an effort to find out something you
didn't know before and to tell someone else about it who
has an interest in it.

The Free Mini-College

A combination of Paul Goodman's idea for mini-schools
and ideas from the free school movement could be used
by departments in the social sciences and the humanities
who authorized a department member to put together a
mini-college of fifty to one hundred students, from freshmen to seniors, or of students drawn from a single class
who volunteered for the program. Space could be taken in
one of the college dormitories as the residential base for
all or part of the free college. One variation might be to
have fifty residents joined together with fifty commuters
so that the commuters would have a base on the campus.

The faculty member would be responsible for the entire educational program of his group for a semester,
and would be free to choose his own staff from faculty
volunteers, graduate students, and undergraduates who
wished to join him in the teaching. The budget for the
free college would be calculated at the regular rate of
per-student cost and faculty-student ratio, with stipends
for graduate students who give half their time to teaching,
the other half to research and study related to the subjects being taught in the free college, for which they
would receive credit toward the degree.

The curriculum would be developed by the students
themselves, together with the faculty leader and staff,
and would be centered in research, study, field work,
seminars, and projects, with possibly one meeting of
the whole college once a week for two hours at which
there would be speakers on various topics, student-faculty or student symposia, question and answer sessions,
business sessions on college affairs, etc. The meetings

would be planned by a student steering committee which would work with the faculty leader in planning the all-college program.

Each student, with the help of the staff, would work out a curriculum for himself for the semester, and would join with other students in teams for research and seminar work. Students could enroll in courses in the regular university program where there seemed relevant to his total plan, and each student's curriculum, with any comments he cared to make about it, would be mimeographed and distributed in a folder along with other material to the rest of the students, so that each would know what the others were doing and could join with them in various projects where this seemed useful to a particular group.

The schedule of meetings both on and off the campus, seminars, research groups, would be worked out by the students, with student members of the free college acting as administrative assistants to the faculty leader, in a college office arranged in one of the dormitory rooms. Many of the other ideas already suggested for student-initiated education would be put into effect—a library of student work (xeroxed or mimeographed, taped or recorded), along with anything else which the free college developed for itself, including its own grading system if it wanted one.

Student Travel

A department could, if it wished, sponsor student travel for study, collaboration, and research throughout the state, using the idea developed by the students who organized the Earth Liberation Front. Four students from East Lansing, Michigan, in January 1970, pooled their resources to buy an unused but usable school bus, repaired it, and fitted it up as a traveling educational laboratory and mobile home. They then set off to visit campuses across the country to collect and distribute ideas and literature to students, teachers, labor unions, community groups—to anyone who had an interest in new projects in education, social change, housing, co-operatives, communes, free universities, film-making, auto mechanics, theater, and dozens of other topics. As they traveled to thirty campuses from East to West, they met people of all kinds with all kinds of ideas, collected from them whatever materials they had, distributed what they had already collected in their wake, having learned from their new friends and having put them in touch with each other.

The students now plan to organize a caravan of four buses to expand the work they have been doing, including (1) a Resource Bus, with workshop material on everything from day care centers to food cooperatives, free schools and existing educational reform projects in colleges; (2) a Multi-Media Bus, with film showings on current events, radio station equipment for campus broadcasting, posters, photography and video tape workshops, crafts and arts supplies, xerography—a bus for showing people what they can do with their own equipment for use in community education; (3) a Book Bus, with packets of reprints, paperbacks, annotated bibliographies, documents like the *Whole Earth Catalogue*, manuals on how to start community and campus projects, records and tapes, mimeographed materials from student and faculty research on environmental problems; and (4) a General Store Bus, which would serve as the commissary for the caravan, as well as give instruction in health foods, nutrition, how to start food cooperatives, nursery schools, child care centers, the use of new kinds of children's playthings, and how to build new playgrounds for children.

The students also propose the use of similar buses with folding stages for student theater and music groups; an auto mechanics bus which would show local students how to build their own bus, repair the engine, fit it up with equipment for similar travel; a bus which would contain the model equipment and plans for building a geodesic dome. Those on the bus would show the local students how to build a dome which could be used as a students' reading room, resource center, and educational workshop. If the idea of taking education and students into the state were sponsored by colleges of education, or departments in the arts and sciences, there is a body of experience already developed by the Earth Liberation Front as well as by existing bookmobile and theater-mobile programs on which the students and faculty could build.

Until now, mobile educational projects have been confined to state health programs and libraries, professional groups in music and theater, transportation of children to school, and football and basketball teams to games. An extension of the idea of mobile education could very well be sponsored by the students and faculty from any one of the departments, at a minimum cost, especially if the travel were considered a part of the education of the students and received academic credit. Where buses were unavailable, cars and station wagons on loan from students and parents could be substituted.

Off-Campus Study Centers

There is a whole range of possibility for action by departments in organizing off-campus study centers, storefront colleges for community children and adults, child care centers, recreation centers and, for example, through collaboration between the biology, sociology, and psychology departments, in organizing community projects in nutrition, health, childrearing, and education, building on the foundations already established by student tutorial programs and community services projects. There could be built-in student research in each case, with courses using the results of the research as well as the general literature in the field of urban studies, as materials for class discussion.

There is no need to extend the examples, since many universities are producing them for themselves through urban studies centers and other applications of university resources to community needs. What is lacking in the approach of the universities is the introduction of the idea of a direct relationship between the community and student learning as part of the responsibility of the departments as they develop their curricula. As of now, educational thinking in the day-to-day work of the departments confines itself almost exclusively to what is done on the campus and in the classrooms.

Adaptation of the Parkway Program

An example for the departments could be drawn from the Parkway Program in Philadelphia, where high school students in study groups of ten to fifteen use the city of Philadelphia as their campus under the guidance of their teachers and choose the studies they will carry on from nearly one hundred course offerings, from law enforcement to modern dance. The program requires no extra school space and no extra teachers, since most of the studying is done in the city at museums, television and radio studios, libraries, government offices, in parents' homes, wherever there is space, and the number of teachers required is the same as the present ratio of students to teachers in the regular classroom arrangements.

Each student and teacher belongs to a tutorial group consisting of fifteen students and a university intern who is learning to be a teacher. The group serves three functions: to act as the central place in which the student does his learning and gets his counselling, to teach the basic skills of language and mathematics, and to serve as the place in which the student's continuing performance is evaluated. There are no numerical or letter grades, the only grade given is a pass, and if a student is unable to function in the work he undertakes, the course does not appear on his transcript. Membership in the Parkway

Program, for both students and teachers, is through volunteering.

Transposed to the university, the Parkway approach sponsored by a single department could substitute the area of study of its own subject matter for the language and mathematics of the Parkway program and count this as credit for half the student's full-time work over a given semester. The high school students in Philadelphia often use the evenings and weekends for the studies they are carrying on, and recruit parents, friends, public officials, musicians—anyone with something to offer to the subjects they are studying.

Internal and External Communes

There is room for serious experiment in applying the idea of the commune or intentional learning centers to all the residential arrangements of the campus by arranging for students within a given department, who are working at a set of common projects, to live together in sections of the dormitories and to make that the base of operations for a semester, with commuting students attached to the group as non-resident members. Students have already started intentional learning centers and communes of their own, most of them outside the university system, but some of them as cooperatives organized by students with common interests who have rented a house and used it as a center for their work as students. Art projects in redesigning the interiors, self-taught courses, seminars, reading and discussion sessions, music, and libraries of student research have all been part of their work together.

As of now, the only systematic way in which the idea of the commune has ever been used on the campuses is by the fraternities and sororities, with the social and educational disadvantage that the inhabitants have come together on racial, economic, and status criteria rather than on a sharing of intellectual and aesthetic interests.

They do provide companionship and a sense of belonging, but to a status group rather than to a learning center.

It is possible that through collaboration among the departments, some of the fraternity and sorority houses could be turned into learning centers, especially in the case of those which are hard-pressed for funds and members and have trouble filling the houses. It would also be possible for the departments to sponsor cooperatives for students and to agree to grant credit for some of the course work the students did together in their residences. The idea is often carried out in the case of students of foreign languages with their language houses, and could be extended into the rest of the curriculum if the departments became interested.

New Cooperative Courses

Another example of possibilities for the departments comes from the work of a group of students and faculty members at the University of Illinois in Urbana, who developed a course in heuristics, in their definition, "the study of the as yet unknown processes by which knowledge is acquired," or in the Webster dictionary definition, "helping to discover or learn: sometimes used to designate a method of education in which the pupil is trained to find out things for himself." Three faculty members were involved originally (from the fields of music, biology and neurophysiology, and electrical engineering), and at first twenty-three, then fifty-two, and finally 156 students, from all ranks and fields. The faculty member in charge was Professor Heinz Von Foerster of electrical engineering and physics.

Taking the general suggestion made by the *Whole Earth Catalogue* published by the Portola Institute of Menlo Park, California, one of the combined class projects of two courses in electrical engineering and one in English called upon the class members to put together a Whole University Catalogue, with each student contributing what he felt might be useful. The ninety-six-page publication which resulted is an extraordinary document; in its preparation the students obviously learned a great deal by being forced to discover things for themselves and to leave behind the conventional ways in which what they had learned could be presented.

The items in the catalogue range from collages of photographs with captions to a page of excerpts from Wittgenstein and directions for playing the University Game, a game constructed in the style of Monopoly. The criticism and comments on the university and the way they are presented make the catalogue one of the funniest and most serious documents now available on the character of the American university. The sponsorship by Professor Von Foerster and his collaborators in other departments indicates one more way in which the university can be reformed from inside.

World Seminars with Foreign Students

There is a wealth of possibilities for departmental sponsorship of programs for foreign students which would use their knowledge of their own countries in seminars and student-run courses to study world affairs from a completely international point of view. As of now on most campuses, the study of non-Western and non-American cultures is centered in area studies programs, or institutes, and education in international affairs is considered a branch of history and political science.

If the idea of internationalism is shifted to the idea of a world society and the world is studied as one society with a variety of cultures in it, the study of world affairs can be conducted with the help of students from foreign countries who add what they know to what the others know. A department of political science, sociology, philosophy, or psychology could organize seminars in world problems in which foreign students, graduates, and undergraduates would be asked to join in the teaching by presenting the point of view of the country or region from which they come.

A general model for such seminars was developed in an experimental project for a world college in 1963 on a small campus in Long Island operated by the Society of Friends, where a completely international student body and faculty worked together in a curriculum which took the major problems of world society—among them ideological conflict, the prevention of war, the maldistribution of wealth and food resources, the peaceful uses of atomic energy—as the starting point for putting together their own materials for study and use.

At the present time, although there are more than one hundred thousand foreign students in the American universities, very little is done to make use of their special knowledge and experience as representatives of other cultures to effect changes in the curriculum or in the teaching program. They too are put through the regulation requirements of an American curriculum, and their potential influence in bringing a world point of view into the American schools and colleges is thereby wasted.[*]

The Revision of Special Sequences

Another contribution the departments could make to the welfare of students would be to eliminate or drastically revise the idea of introductory, intermediate, and advanced courses which are the basis for the sequences of courses leading to graduation in a field of specialty. Along with this would be eliminated the idea that everything is prerequisite to everything else and that the B.A. major in a given field is simply a prerequisite for graduate school. If the undergraduate subject matter requirements

[*] Harold Taylor, *The World As Teacher* (New York: Doubleday, 1969) contains an extended discussion of the world college idea and its possibilities for use on the American campuses.

are removed, the graduate school requirements will have to be changed. Otherwise the graduate schools would be unable to accept the best students.

The introductory courses are just that; they introduce the student to the subject matter of a given discipline instead of plunging him into the study itself. Most of the introductory courses are not a necessary prelude to what comes afterward, except in the sense that there may be some words in the academic vocabulary which must be defined and recognized, certain concepts which must become familiar. Most of these can be dealt with fairly quickly by means other than taking a full course in them. The freshman student who is interested in biology or psychology or anthropology should have a chance to go directly into classes with students of other years. There is no particular magic in being a junior which compels a department to keep him apart from freshman or seniors.

It is because so many departmental courses are locked into a sequence that demands coverage of certain material in orderly succession that the student accusations of irrelevancy become valid. A course that is relevant to the purpose of preparing a student to take a next course may be relevant to that purpose and to no other.

17. Natural Change

An illustrative list of projects of the kind I have described could go on and on, with ideas taken from reports on what is already happening, from the literature in the field of educational change, and most of all, from anyone, anywhere in any department in any college or university who cares to work out projects with his students. There should be more communication among faculty members, inside their own universities as well as between institutions, about what is being done in teaching, and I wish more university teachers would write about their classes and let their colleagues know about changes being made in style and content.*

The confessional writing of teachers in the schools—John Holt, Jonathan Kozol, James Herndon, George Dennison, and others—has not yet found its counterpart among university teachers who have written mainly as sociologists and social scientists about the student revolts at Berkeley, Columbia, Harvard, and elsewhere, but not as teachers in the regular course of their work with students. Once there is more interest inside the departments in educational change, we can look for a whole new literature of this kind, both from the teachers and the students.

Once the students become part of the course-making and the teaching, they lend themselves naturally to the extension of the work of the course into broader areas of the campus. I remember at one point in the program of teaching in the philosophy department at the University of Wisconsin in the early 1940's that two members of the faculty, who had raised some questions in their courses about the existence of God in relation to the beliefs of humanists, found themselves with a dozen

* Most readers are probably familiar with the magazine *Change* which serves as one way of exchanging information among university and college teachers about changes going on in their work.

out of the two or three hundred students in the courses who wanted to continue the study of the questions for the rest of the term. The faculty members suggested that the students themselves take on that part of the course outside the regular sessions, offered to help them, and a new organization called Vanguard, devoted to the discussion of religious questions, was formed by the dozen students, with bi-weekly meetings attracting five and six hundred students to hear debates and discussion on subjects ranging from the difference between Freud's and Tillich's views of the self to the contradictions in St. Thomas's doctrine of the freedom of the will. A lot of first-rate education went on without the department doing anything more than sponsoring it.

Once they become committed to an interest in the educational policies and planning in a given department, students are also likely to become very helpful in working with faculty members on all the details of course arrangements and programs which the departments care to sponsor. In most of the cases where departments have taken the kind of responsibility I have been suggesting for acting as educational planners, the students have joined in as informal assistants in carrying out the plans. In many cases they have been the first to suggest the plans.

In a sense, this amounts to a transposition of what already goes on when students organize their own conferences and programs *against* the university. But in this case, no matter how seriously they may disagree with university policy or with the departments on other matters, they cannot disagree about doing something they want to do and have agreed to do. The criticism some students have made of student-faculty internal colleges in the departments is that they are simply a more sophisticated way of co-opting the students into a state of educational acquiescence. The answer is that if under the new arrangement the student is getting the kind of education he has been fighting for, he needs some other word than co-optation to describe what has happened to him.

The role of the department chairman in all this is crucial. There are some departments where a man with serious educational ideas could not be elected chairman. In most others where a lucky situation exists—a liberal-minded dean who has power of appointment, an educator as chairman of the department, and enough department members who want to make educational changes—almost all the things that need to be done can be done, from revising the grading system to changing the content of the curriculum. If this kind of departmental initiative and cooperative attitude toward students had been taken long ago in developing a new kind of intellectual life inside the universities, we would not now find our-selves with a university system so stubbornly resistant to change. The changes would have come year by year as circumstances warranted and new needs became ev-ident. The problems would have remained, but there would have been a ready-made structure in which to work at their solution.

A shift of the kind I am proposing would also have a direct effect on the development of teachers for the col-leges, the universities, and the public schools. When students are asked, in effect, to become their own teach-ers, and there are specific ways in which they are asked to help in making educational policy, the concept of teaching as a special skill to be learned in separate bouts of "practice teaching" is eliminated in favor of the idea of teaching as a way of helping others to learn. One of the things which is bound to be missing as the present system works is a chance for the student to understand education itself. The average undergraduate and grad-uate student never has a chance to learn about education

and its place in society except through what he reads in
the papers, hears from student activists, or sees in films
or on television.

As of now, most students accept as truth what they
hear about education from other student activists. For
the most part it matches their own experience. But they
are seldom well enough informed to be able to think their
way through to independent conclusions about how to
change the system. They have had no stimulus to do so
unless they join the opposition. That may of course be
as good a place as any to make a beginning, but what
is needed is not only a beginning but a next stage and a
stage after that in which their involvement in educational reform finally becomes perfectly natural by reason
of their practical experience in teaching themselves and
one another.

When there is a student-faculty educational policies
committee of some kind in each department as well as
general student participation in teaching in the courses,
not only does the student attitude to teaching change but
many more of the most interesting students are recruited
into teaching. They and their fellow students form part of
a new body of informed educational opinion of much
larger size than we have ever had before, and student
radicals, activists, and militants then have to take account
of a much larger and better informed constituency for
their ideas, but at the same time can count on more help
in pressing for reforms which can win the approval of
the wider constituency. Too often as things now stand,
the number of radical critics is not matched by a large
enough number of radical planners, and some of the over-
simplified descriptions and denunciations of "the system"
merely serve as clichés to satisfy the market for radical
clichés rather than as a basis for serious reform.

It is my hope that beginning now, in this period of
American educational crisis, the university will turn

back to the primary task from which its attention has
been distracted for so many years—the task of teaching
students. I realize that there are many who will tell me
that the crisis on the campuses is one which is driving
faculty members away from students, and that the controversy, the disruptions, the daily and yearly turmoil,
which has now become normal on so many campuses, are
making it impossible to enjoy the life of the university
scholar, and that the gap between students and their
teachers is now so great that it can no longer be closed.
I have been told that the most that can be done is to try
to restore order to the chaos and hope that one of these
days it will be possible to resume the even tenor of civilized discourse which is the characteristic of the true
university environment.

It is just possible that that day will never come again,
at least until the idea of what is civilized and what is un-
civilized is redefined. The need for quiet, for calm, for
a peaceful center to one's life, for relief from the pressures of a modern world which seems bent on destroying
the best that is in man—these are needs which somehow
must be met, not merely for university scholars and the
intellectuals of the world, but for those to whom peace
of mind is an impossible fantasy because of the impov-
erishment of the spirit imposed on them by the physical
conditions of their existence.

We have reached a point in human history at which no
matter what happens, we are all in it together and there
is no place to hide. The university is and must be a
sanctuary where the human intellect is protected and
cherished, but the intellect may not be hidden there. It
is now a public property, owned by the human race, and
its fruits must be shared by all in need of them. If there
are disorders and troubles on the way to that sharing,
it is some comfort to know that the disorders are part
of an historical process. Whether we can work our way
through this transitional period and come out the other

side has a great deal to do with how we use the massive intellectual resources of the world's universities, and whether we can find a way of coming to terms with the needs and demands of the next generation in history. We are reminded every day that the needs are there, and the demands. It is time to be very practical, and without the apportionment of blame, without the use of force, to design a new environment for learning in which everyone has a chance to enjoy the quality of life that true learning makes possible.

Lewis and Clark College - Watzek Library

LB2322 .T29   wmain
Taylor, Harold/How to change colleges: n

3 5209 00417 6968